NO-INFLUENCE MENTORING

Understanding teenagers and encouraging their success

Jacob Kashiwagi, Ph.D.

No-Influence Mentoring, Copyright © 2020 by Jacob Kashiwagi. All Rights Reserved.

All rights reserved. No part of this book may be reproduced in any form or by any electronic or mechanical means including information storage and retrieval systems, without permission in writing from the author. The only exception is by a reviewer, who may quote short excerpts in a review.

Cover design by Jake A. Gunnoe and Nguyen Le

Edited by Katie Chambers | Beacon Point Services
Edited by Jake A. Gunnoe | Leadership Society of Arizona

The views expressed in this report are based solely on the independent research performed by the author. This publication does not necessarily represent the views of any of the partners or participating groups mentioned in this research.

Jacob Shizuo Kashiwagi
Connect with me at www.LinkedIn.com/in/JacobKashiwagi
Email me at: Team@LeadAZ.org

Produced and distributed by Leadership Society of Arizona, 501(c)(3).

Printed first in the United States of America
First Edition Spring 2020
KSM, Inc.
ISBN: 978-0-9985836-8-6

Table of Contents

1	Adjusting the Paradigm of Learning	1
2	The Challenge of Being a Child	11
3	What Do Leaders Look Like?	22
4	No-Influence Mentoring	45
5	Individual Centered	53
6	Simplicity Structured	71
7	Action Focused	83
8	A Framework of Natural Laws	101
9	Conclusion	119
	Research History	123
	About the Author	130
	Staying Involved	133

—A Special Invitation—

Welcome to the No-Influence community!

As you will soon find out by reading this book, No-Influence Mentoring is a unique approach to helping people find **confidence**, **happiness**, and **purpose**. This extends well beyond teenagers. I have been using No-Influence methods in the home, workplace, and classroom for over 20 years. My hope is that this book will serve multiple purposes for you:
1. Help you improve interactions with teenagers in your life.
2. Introduce you to a new way of thinking about leadership, management, and mentoring

My passion is helping others. I want to help you be successful at whatever makes you happy. So, if you like this book, I invite you to join me and other parents, teachers, and professionals in our unique community of people who love to help others.

Here's how to get involved:
1. You can sign up for my **FREE online course**, No-Influence Mentoring. It provides videos and activities to go along with this book. Visit LeadAZ.org/NIM
2. Join our **Facebook Group** and post your thoughts about the book: Facebook.com/Groups/ParentLeadership
3. **Email me** with questions, comments, or feedback at Team@LeadAZ.org.

For access to my free course and other materials visit:

LeadAZ.org/NIM

1
Adjusting the Paradigm of Learning
Kids don't need teachers; they need mentors

Introduction

Since the creation of what we now call education and the school system, society and the world has changed. Education was originally started by religious groups wanting to increase people's faith in God. This led to communities wanting to use education to train better citizens and soldiers. Then the industrial revolution changed education to ensure that it could develop better workers. At that time, most jobs consisted of manual labor or some type of technical skill repeated over and over. The industry needed people who could follow directions; very few jobs required leadership skills or creativity. With the development of the computer, internet, and advanced technology, all of this changed. Most manual labor and technical positions are being eliminated. Recently, Amazon started automating analytics-based jobs in their company and replacing them with computer technology[1]. Moving into the future, most available positions will require leadership, innovation, and ingenuity.

Thus, to prepare kids for the future, education will have to change, but not just in schools. All education, both formal and informal must change. Every adult responsible for children must change with the times. The current paradigm of education does not teach children relevant professional skills, and it doesn't develop the right characteristics in children to become successful. Our education system is not geared toward creating leaders, it is geared toward molding a person who will need to be told what to do, how to do it, and when to do it their whole life. It teaches them to be reactive, to wait until someone tells them what to do.

Starting at age seven (in some cases even earlier), a child will go to a place that tells them what to learn, how to learn it, and when to learn it. The structure of the school day dictates the majority of their day and what they will need to do. Then they go home and their family often dictates what they do outside of education. Thus, most of the child's interaction with adults will be someone telling the child what they "should" be doing. This usually continues until the child is around sixteen–eighteen. In many cases, the child will then go to college for another four years. That gives them some freedom but still follows the same educational format. You can probably guess the result of a child being told what to do for twenty-two years. They continue to wait for instructions, needing to be told what to do their entire life.

We need to transition from *creating* dependent adults to enabling independent adults. I have seen many children fail because they don't know how to live their own lives. They have been told what to do so often, they no longer can make their own decisions.

College and the industry show this with their reported statistics:
1. One-third of college students change majors[2]
2. 49 percent of students are in jobs unrelated to their major[3]
3. 87 percent of recent grads are unsatisfied with their job[4]
4. 40 percent of students drop out of college[5]
5. 89 percent of employers think recent grads do not have the right skillsets to succeed in their company[6]

If this is a shock to you, then brace yourself because it is going to get much worse. The fact that education trains students to become reactive followers is only the beginning.

To really understand the gravity of the situation, you need to sit back and ask, "What should children get out of education and their childhood? Why is it important for children to receive an education?" You will probably come to the following two conclusions:
1. It should help the children learn to live a life that makes them happy.
2. It should help the children identify and learn how to be good citizens and add value to society.

If you have the best interest of children at heart and think logically, you will have the same conclusions. All parents want their children to grow up and get good jobs (one that earns good money), be a good person (be a person others like to be around and can fit into society), and be happy (enjoy what they are doing and their life). That is what life is about. Everyone needs to learn how to get along with others, enjoy what they are doing, and find a way to earn a living by adding value.

Unfortunately, this is not the purpose of education. Today, the sole purpose of the school system is to ensure all children attain a certain technical level of understanding, so they are prepared to go to college. To make matters worse, since education has such a big influence on society, it is changing the way parents define success for their children. Most parents believe their main goal should be to make sure their kids do well in school—happiness comes later.

The issue is that technical education and finishing college don't determine happiness or your ability to add value to society. This has been proven with many research studies[7]. In other words, education today is making life about learning technical information, taking tests, and going to college when it should be about learning how to add value to society, being happy, and becoming successful.

In fact, I have met many people who have become very successful without going to college. I have a very good friend who is a computer programmer. He taught himself how to write code, and now he has his own business and makes more money than most people I know who went to college. If you look at the richest people in the world today, you also find that many of them didn't graduate from college (Bill Gates, Christy Walton, Ingvar Kamprad, Liliane Bettencourt, Michael Dell, etc.). Not that college and test-taking is a "bad" thing, it is just not the purpose of life. Of course, many people who went to college have become successful. But when students shape their life around scoring well on a test, it ends up being detrimental to them when they no longer live in a school environment.

The impact of focusing on teaching children technical information and requiring them to meet certain standards shows how detrimental the current education system is to mental health as well:
- Suicide is the second leading cause of death for US citizens ages ten to thirty-four.[8]
- In 2017 suicides among teen girls hit a forty-year high.[9]
- Between 2010 and 2015, teen depression increased by 33 percent.[10]
- In the same period, teen suicide increased by 31 percent.[10]
- About one-third of US college students had difficulty functioning in the last twelve months because of depression and half felt "overwhelming anxiety."[11]
- 70 percent of teens say that anxiety and depression are a "major problem."[12]
- Daily anxiety can often lead to more serious cases of depression or other mental health disorders.[13]

Amazingly, the demand on students to learn such a high technical level of understanding causes all the issues. Life has become more complex. The amount of information a child must learn today compared to a hundred years ago is mind-boggling. This is the issue with what I call the top-down approach: when we inundate children with as many technical details as we can, hoping that we will teach them enough to understand the world and know what they want to do after they graduate. However, teaching an inexperienced child a lot of information at once stresses them out and confuses them. Imagine a small plastic bag; it can only fit so much in it before it starts to break. This is much like the human brain. It can only fit so much information in it before it breaks down. However, if the bag breaks, you then get a bigger bag to carry what you need, whereas the brain doesn't get any bigger or more advanced. It is the same human brain, yet we are still trying to put way more information in it, and you can see the stress it is taking now. I also need to be clear that the amount of information a person needs to know to be successful is well within the limits of what a brain can take.

No matter how much we try to reshape, repackage, or even automate the learning of the information, the issues will continue to get worse. The only way to help the children is to change it.

No-Influence Mentoring

The No-Influence Mentoring model is based on ancient philosophy. The ideas and practices have been known for thousands of years. They have been understood and used by all the greatest minds in history and in every industry and aspect of life (Socrates, Isaac Newton, Albert Einstein, Mahatma Gandhi, W. Edwards Deming, Eleanor Roosevelt, James Allen, and more). Anyone required to deal with people and who has become successful in their discipline has used some or all the practices found in this book. You might even find that you already use some of these practices in your own style of teaching, mentoring, or parenting.

For many, this model will seem new. This is only because I am exposing it at a time when the current practices are either opposed to or are very different from it. I am also bringing many successful ideas from multiple areas outside of the academic and the education environment.

My expertise did not originate in teaching and leading young students. It began in process engineering, moved to construction management, and then shifted into business and supply chain management. Yet for the last twenty years, I have been studying and testing these techniques not only in educating youth but applying them to multiple organizations and professionals all over the world. I am still involved in consulting with professional organizations and companies.

You might ask, "Why did I shift my interest into getting involved with education?" It is simple: education has more impact on society. Fixing problems in the industry without addressing the root cause is like trying to help the poor by giving them food. It helps them for a day, but it doesn't solve the problem. They will need more food later. There is a saying: *you can't teach an old dog new tricks*. This could not be truer. When someone has been taught all their life to live and act a certain way or to do business a certain way, it is extremely hard to get them to change. Trying to get a fifty-five-year-old professional to change their ways is like trying to potty train a five-month-old baby. It is extremely messy and takes a lot of effort, and in the end, they still will not be potty trained. Education has the potential to help children learn the right way when they are young and ensure they know how to get their own food.

Amazingly, the issues the industry is facing with their employees are the same issues that parents and teachers are facing with students and children.

This model is as much for parents as it is for teachers because education starts in the home or family. The only reason education can continue to operate the way it does is because parents accept/promote it. In order for teachers and schools to make the required change, parents must also understand that grades, test scores, and getting into the top universities is not the purpose of life. Yes, these things might help children, but they are not the purpose of their life.

No-Influence mentoring will not only help teachers teach students better but will also help parents to raise and educate more stable children.

The Purpose of Education

Education should develop students so they can become happy, healthy, responsible, and value-adding citizens. Sometimes we forget this. We get so involved in math, English, or a million other things we want to teach the kids and forget why we are teaching them these subjects. We now live in an age where even adults feel like if a child is not active and being exposed to something every second of the day, they are not going to be prepared for the future. They fill their children's time so much, the children no longer know what to do when someone hasn't filled their time. And they are so busy with things that they never figure out what they really want to do. And all the while their brain is slowly filling up, being strained, and sometimes even breaks.

We don't teach these subjects and keep our children busy for no reason. It was determined that these things can help a child's life. However, the issue is we became more focused on *subjects* and curriculum than on the students' *lives*. Education is not about preparing a student for college or a job; education is about preparing a student for life. I try to remind leaders, don't work to stay busy; work to add value.

In many cases, teachers and parents fear that if they don't focus on the curriculum or introduce children to diverse experiences, their children will not do well academically or professionally, and they will not have value. I propose that when a student is happy, not stressed, and supported by the teacher and parents, they will perform better, learn more, and the teachers and parents won't have to do as much.

The times have changed. There are so many avenues to provide value to society. In many cases, students do not need to meet the standards in math, English, history, economics, or science, or be exposed to every type of occupation to be successful and provide value to society.

We need a system that focuses on the child and student. We need parents and teachers who want to be mentors and not just managers. We need leaders.

Conclusion

The purpose of this book is not to instruct you on *what to do*. It is to provide you with correct concepts and ideas that will enable you to identify how you need to change to become more of a leader for your children. There is no "right" way to lead; everyone will naturally do things differently, but every leader follows the same correct principles.

Becoming a leader is not easy. It requires personal development. And even though many will tell you there is a step-by-step process for it, there isn't. Everyone is different, so each person will have to figure out how to develop and incorporate these correct leadership principles into their life their own way.

I can tell you that it is worth it. It is also the only way to provide your children or students with an atmosphere and support system that will enable them to develop into happy, stable, and productive people.

Chapter Summary and Goals

Making the needed changes will not come through repeating physical actions over and over, it will occur through greater understanding. If you desire to take the first step to changing, you can take the following actions to develop a greater understanding:
1. Do your own research on what makes people successful and the characteristics and attributes of people you would like your children and students to be like.
2. Do your own research on the education system. The more you know what is happening and the impact it is having on people, the more strength and determination you will have to make the change.
3. Talk with your children or students. The more you talk with them about their views and opinions, the more you will figure out a change is needed.
4. Reflect on your own life and education. Review in your own life what has helped you to obtain success or what has brought you the things that are most meaningful in your life.

Good luck on your journey! I hope that you will keep up your hope, motivation, and drive. Your effort will enable you to support your children/students and develop stronger relationships with them. For more activities, check out my free course by visiting LeadAZ.org/NIM.

[1] Dave Gershon, Amazon has already begun automating its white-collar jobs, (Quartz, 2018)
[2] National Center for Education Statistics, *Beginning College Students Who Change Their Majors Within 3 Years of Enrollment* (U.S. Department of Education, 2017).
[3] Hunt, R., *51 Percent of Employed 2014 College Grads Are in Jobs That Don't Require a Degree, Finds CareerBuilder Survey* (CareerBuilder Press Release, 2014).
[4] Forbes, *Millennials Will Soon Rule the World. How Will The Lead?* (Forbes 2013).
[5] U.S. Department of Education, National Center for Education Statistics, *The Condition of Education 2019* (NCES, 2019, 144).
[6] Gallup, *What America Needs to Know About Higher Education Redesign*, (Higher Education, 2014)
[7] Susan Adams, *Unhappy Employees Outnumber Happy Ones By Two To One Worldwide*, (Forbes, 2013).
[8] Hedegaard, H., Curtin, S., Warner, *Suicide Mortality in the United States, 1999–2017*, (National Center for Health Statistics, 2018).
[9] Fox, M. *Suicides in Teen Girls Hit 40-Year High*, (NBC News, 2017).
[10] Twenge, J. M., Joiner, T. E., Rogers, M. L., & Martin, G. N., *Increases in Depressive Symptoms, Suicide-Related Outcomes, and Suicide Rates Among U.S. Adolescents After 2010 and Links to Increased New Media Screen Time*, (Clinical Psychological Science, 2018), 6(1), 3–17.
[11] Novotney A. *Students under pressure*, (American Psychology Association, 2014), (45) (8).
[12] Graf, N., Horowitz, J., *Most U.S. Teens See Anxiety and Depression as a Major Problem Among Their Peers*, (Pew Research Center, 2019)
[13] McCarthy, C., *Anxiety in Teens is Rising: What's Going On?* (American Academy of Pediatrics, 2019).

2
The Challenge of Being a Child

Are Children Becoming Worse?

The common belief among most parents, teachers, and news outlets is that children are getting worse as time moves on. With every generation, it seems that children expect more, desire to do less, have less discipline, less motivation, and are less capable.

The following quote aptly describes the modern opinion:

> "The children now love luxury; they have bad manners, contempt for authority; they show disrespect for elders and love chatter in place of exercise."[1]

Ironically, this quote is attributed to Socrates in reference to the children in Athens, Greece, around 300 B.C. In reality, it seems that historically the older generations always look at the younger generations and believe they are getting worse. People throughout history have complained about the previous generation:

1. Hesiod (800 BC)—"I see no hope for the future . . . for certainly all youth are **reckless** beyond words. When I was young, we were taught to be **discreet** and respectful of elders, but the present youth are exceedingly **disrespectful** and **impatient** of restraint."[2]

2. Peter the Hermit (1200 AD)—"The young people of today **think of nothing but themselves**. They have **no respect** for their parents or old age. They are **impatient** of all restraint."[3]
3. Granville Stanley Hall (1904)—"Never has youth been exposed to such dangers of both **perversion** and arrest as in our own land and day. Increasing urban life with its **temptations**, prematurities, **sedentary occupations**, and **passive stimuli** . . ."[4]

Technology is often blamed for the degradation of the future generation. This hasn't changed. Socrates would go on to say the following about the development and increased use of writing, the technology of their time:

> "[Writing] will create forgetfulness in the learners' souls, because they will not use their memories; they will trust to the external written characters and not remember of themselves... they will be hearers of many things and will have learned nothing; they will appear to be omniscient and will generally know nothing."[5]

I have seen many news articles claiming that smartphones and the internet are ruining children's ability to pay attention and learn. When I was younger, it used to be computers; they were making it so children couldn't handwrite things anymore.

The older generation always fears for the next, but reality shows their fears are not warranted. Over time, society has been able to develop better technology, produce more, and become more efficient. Society has also become more accepting over time (as seen with the abolishment of slavery and improved treatment of minority groups).

It seems like the biggest issues have nothing to do with the younger generation; instead, the biggest issues are with the older generation coming to grips with the changes that modern-day advancements are bringing to society.

This is the same issue that is occurring in families and classrooms today. When the older generation was growing up (if you didn't realize this yet, the older generation is you and me), the way people learned and what they valued was different than today. However, teachers and parents are still trying to teach the youth the same way and are focusing on the same ideas. This might be why many children do not want to focus on school. With open access to any information that they want, youth have become very smart. They know when something doesn't make sense. They can quickly tell when they are being asked to do something that doesn't match with requirements to be successful. Not only that but they can also now learn from the brightest minds on the planet whenever they want, and they just need their smartphone to do it. Is it no wonder so many students can't pay attention in class or get bored?

The Biggest Issue Children Face

Over the last ten years, I have taught thousands of college and high school students and have mentored hundreds of parents and children. From that experience, I found the biggest and most common issue students face is living up to the expectations of adults. It could be their parents, family, teachers, or even a club leader.

Amazingly, whenever I have dealt with students and their parents, the students usually have a sincere desire to live up to their parents' expectations, but they just don't know how. Then I talk with the parents, and they express how their children just don't seem to understand the importance or have the desire to do better.

Too often, adults overestimate what a student can do, which eventually affects the student's life. I have seen track coaches push athletes to run faster than their health allows, math teachers recommend students be placed in higher math classes than they can handle, and parents push their children into more difficult programs or schools. Unfortunately, I have also seen children whose bodies were ruined before they got to college; students who struggled to pass math classes, thinking they just weren't smart; and students who learned to hate school. This is not the most uplifting idea I get to talk about, but it is very real. It gets worse when you see the number of students who sink into depression and are medicated for stress, worry, anxiety, and fear. All because of unrealistic expectations. The number of children who have nervous breakdowns, suicidal thoughts, and/or can't sleep at night has been increasing exponentially over the last ten years.

Often the adults leave no room for being wrong. We assume that we know exactly who someone is, what it will take for them to be successful, and what they are capable of doing. We also seem to think we have an uncanny ability to know when it's the right time for a child to change. It is rare for an adult to stop and think, "What if I am wrong? What if I have unrealistic expectations or I have under- or overestimated the skill of this child?"

Because they don't stop to think about it and just plow ahead, these assumptions can lead to many issues with both the adult trying to deal with the students and the students being able to develop themselves. Sir Kenneth Robinson, a prominent educator in the United Kingdom, identified many of the issues these assumptions create. He gives the example of two of the Beatles, Paul McCartney and George Harrison, who were in the same music class in grade school with a teacher who did not believe either had any musical talent. Luckily, they still pursued their musical careers. And Elvis Presley who wasn't allowed in the glee club, because they felt he would ruin their sound. Jim Morrison, the lead singer for the band The Doors, left his home and separated from his family, because his father said he would never amount to anything. Tragically, he took his own life at the age of twenty-seven.

Unfortunately, this happens all the time. Both teachers and parents assume they know what will make children successful or what is of value in society. And history has proven that adults are very often wrong.

I remember when I was in ninth grade, I slept all the time in my English class. You can probably guess I wasn't the teacher's favorite. It didn't help that I called her a micro-managing control-freak in my descriptive essay. Yes, I deserved all the pain she took me through. Long story short, eventually my parents had to demand that the school put me in another English class. During this battle, the teacher let my parents know that I would never amount to anything in life and that I didn't have the intellect to make it through college. Luckily, I had good parents and I was cocky in my youth—her comments had no effect on me. Twenty years later, a little wiser, and a lot humbler, I have a bachelor's in industrial engineering, a master's in construction management, and a PhD in supply chain management. Who would have thought?

The truth was, I did sleep through her class. It wasn't that I wanted to, I just wasn't capable of staying awake. And the problem of falling asleep was more complicated than I, or anyone else, realized at the time. Everyone thought it was a choice—I only had to stay awake. Now looking back, I realize, it stemmed from my poor sleeping habits, a serious lack of nutrition, a poor understanding of English concepts, and a teenager trying to figure out what life was about. Some of the issues one could say weren't even my fault; I was just ignorant. But no one explained it to me like this at the time. In fact, at one point I even thought it was a choice.

I remember that every day during lunch I would go into the speech and debate classroom, find a presentation room that was empty, close the door, and sleep for forty-five minutes. I did it so much that one day the speech and debate instructor asked me if I had a health problem. At the time, I laughed and thought it was funny that she thought something was wrong with me. But now, looking back, she probably was right; I probably did have something wrong with me. I wasn't sleeping enough at home, eating right, or maybe I had another chemical imbalance.

This happens a lot in the school system. The biggest expectation students have to overcome is the school system's expectations that they have to receive a high score on standardized tests or get good grades in order to ensure success. From there, many children feel pressure to get into an Ivy League college, get into a specific degree program, or go into a certain occupation. Both of my parents are

Japanese. For Asians there are only three occupations: an engineer, doctor, or a lawyer. If an Asian child wants to be a comedian, dancer, or cook, too bad; those occupations don't even exist.

Reality is very different. Many of the richest people in the world never go to college. When researchers studied millionaires, they found that the average grade they received in school was a C[6]. Add to that the fact that many people have become very successful, value-adding citizens through jobs you would never expect, such as professional Yo-yo entertainer, dog walker and trainer, yard worker, house cleaner, window cleaner, online makeup blogger and YouTuber, travel blogger, food taster, etc. Most of these careers were never taught in school and many parents would laugh at children for wanting to pursue these jobs. Imagine if your child told you that they would make lots of money by people paying them to vacation at the best resorts in the world and blogging about it. It's hard to believe, but many people do it today!

In fact, the school system has the highest expectations for students. To do well, the child must have the following characteristics:
1. Above-average IQ—Learning advanced concepts at a young age.
2. Strong home support system—The amount of homework, classes, and materials they need to keep track of is almost impossible for a child to do alone, especially if they are living in an environment that is loud, requires them to take care of siblings, or work.
3. The ability to sit still for hours—Students remain sitting between –four–six hours during an average school day.

4. A good sleeping schedule—Students must stay alert and have their mind awake when learning in class.
5. Organizational skills and good note-taking—Students must write down the important things a teacher says and keep it in an organized fashion to be able to use it to study for the test.
6. Must be good at all major subjects and memorizing—Students will have to take multiple years of language, math, English, sciences, sports, etc. In each of these classes, they will be required to learn the verbiage and intricacies of the subject.
7. Incredible self-control—The amount of time and effort required to do well in school for a child is often more than a full-time job. The child is expected to put it first above so many other temptations that are more entertaining, enjoyable, and enticing.

For a child to do well in school without stressing, they must have a high IQ, a stable environment, maturity, self-control, and organizational skills. When I look at this list, I don't know of many people in the professional workforce that have all those characteristics, much less know of a child that can do it.

Why Do Adults Have Unrealistic Expectations?

There is a big disconnect between what adults want children to care about and what children actually care about. The parent wants the child to be concerned about their future occupation and life. Hence, the emphasis is placed on memorizing technical information and developing good leadership and life skills. Yet the only reason the parent feels this way is because of their years of experience and understanding of life. People can only care about things that they see. A parent can usually see farther into the future because their brain is fully developed, and they have lived through most everything a child could go through, and much more.

However, children lack experience and understanding, so they can only see what is happening that day or, for more advanced children, maybe one or two months ahead. This vision is limited to entertainment (mainly video games), their schoolwork for that day, sports, socializing, and dealing with their family. They have no vision of what will happen that year, much less twenty years into their future. Having taught thousands of high school and college students, we have found this to be true. Adults forget this. Adults forget when they were children and they didn't have twenty-thirty years of experience. We forget how much time we wasted and what we really cared about when we were a child. Despite having been children once, amazingly most of us have no idea what it is like to be a child. We forget how difficult waking up at six in the morning was or listening to our parents trying to teach us something. But most importantly, we forget how much time we wasted. We forget we weren't busy 24/7. We forget that despite all the time we wasted and the stupid things we did, we still became very successful.

The issue is that if you try to force someone to do something when they can't see its value, they won't learn effectively. On the contrary, many learn to dislike whatever it is they are being forced to do and have no motivation to try. And if they don't, they may obsess over meeting their parents' and teachers' expectations and become overwhelmed with too much technical information. In these cases, they get confused, stressed, and worried about everything because they have so little experience and understanding of life.

When I was teaching at Arizona State University (ASU), the biggest issue I found with honors students is that they can't sleep at night. They can't shut their minds off because of all the stress they have in their lives. Many times, this stress could be coming from disinterest in their degree program or not knowing what they wanted to do with their life. Sometimes the stress would even come from imaginary expectations they thought their parents had on them.

I remember a student from India who had a traumatic experience. Afterward, he went into depression and became fearful and started failing classes. He came to me to explain why he wasn't in class. He was surprised with the support I gave him. He didn't want to tell his parents at first because he felt they would be disappointed. When he finally called them, he couldn't believe the support he received. But the question is: Why didn't he realize his parents would support him? This misperception often stems from the pressure felt throughout his life, to be more than who he is.

Many parents place high expectations on children because of the education system. For years, the education system has put out information convincing adults that the way their children are being educated and evaluated is perfectly reasonable.

The system convinces parents that children need to be developed. This is understandable since they are young. You don't look at an eighty-year-old man and think, "I need to develop him," but when you see a young child walk through the door, naturally you feel an obligation to help them grow, especially if that student is your child.

Developing someone means that you will take them from their current state and change them into something else or help them to another state. To do this, you must have a vision of the future state you are helping them get to. However, when you look into the future, it often causes you to focus more on the future state than the present state.

This is a major issue with adults. They are able to see value in who a child will be, could be, or should be but do not see the value in who a child is today. Adults find themselves caught up in developing the child and seem to always be looking into the future for the child, instead of understanding who the child is right now and what the child enjoys right now. The parent and child end up missing out on the best years of their lives. They tend to replace memories of strengthening their relationships, being happy, and enjoying each other for memories of arguments, stress, and regrets.

Conclusion

This is an important chapter because it highlights the biggest change parents and teachers must make. If we want to minimize the issues our children and students are facing, we need to decrease our expectations. This is not a popular idea, but it is the truth.

The reason schools can never find an effective system is because they have always misdiagnosed the problem. It is impossible to find a solution to an unknown issue. Educators believe that in order to fix the system, we need to "fix" the children. In reality, the issue is the *system*, not the children. There is nothing wrong with children. The children are perfect just the way they are. When developing a community, you must build around the river instead of trying to change its course. This is the same with parents and teachers. Instead of trying to change children, we must adjust everything else to allow them to keep moving. While there are a great many things that we might not be able to change right now, if parents and teachers can change how they look at children and students, that might be enough.

The next chapter will help you to change from this paradigm of expectations to a paradigm that will enable students to grow into confident, productive, and happy adults.

Actions

In this chapter, we identified the greatest issue children face: adults' expectations. In your quest to be a better mentor and leader to your children and students, you also must adjust your expectations to better understand your students/children. You can take the following actions to do this:
1. Talk with someone much older than you regarding the expectations you should have on children. Preferably someone that has grey hair or no hair, that has been successful in life and in raising children. It is important to talk with a person that has been a successful leader.
2. Talk with students/children about what they care about and if they feel any pressure from adults.
3. Research what is being said about younger generations and what was said about your generation when you were young.

4. Look at records and documentation of what you did when you were younger. Talk with your parents or past teachers of what they thought of you when you were young.

In doing the above actions, the hope is that it helps you realize the disconnect adults have with children. That after years of development, adults forget the capability and the difficulties children go through at those ages of development. For more activities, visit my free course at LeadAZ.org/NIM

---

[1] William L. Patty and Louise S. Johnson, *Personality and Adjustment*, (McGraw-Hill, 1953), 277.
[2] This quote is commonly attributed to Hesiod online, but some dispute the original source
[3] This source is also disputed. Some sources attribute it to Socrates and others to a sermon from Peter the Hermit.
[4] Hall GS, *The Psychology of Adolescence*, (D Appleton and Company, New York, NY, 1904).
[5] Plato, Alexander Nehamas, and Paul Woodruff. *Phaedrus*. (Hackett, Indianapolis, IN, 1995).
[6] Eric Barker, *Barking up the Wrong Tree*, (HarperOne, 2017).

3
What Do Leaders Look Like?
Becoming a mentor

Teach without Teaching

Very few people develop their expertise to a point that they become a household name. However, Bruce Lee did this. Not only was he recognized for his martial arts movies, but he also is one of the most respected fighters that has ever lived. He was voted as one of the 100 most influential people of the 20th century by *Time* magazine.[1]

Bruce Lee's fighting style was unique at the time because he believed you should never go against nature and the natural motion of things. His famous words were "Be like water." Water always follows nature; it shapes to whatever it encounters. Usually, if someone threw a punch at you, your natural reaction would be to try to block it—to resist. Bruce Lee realized instead of resisting the force, it's better to allow the punch to take its **course**. Without the resistance, the attacker will **lose** balance and fall over. In other words, your opponent's force will destroy themselves. Instead of trying to resist people, you must adjust yourself to move with them. In *Enter the Dragon*, Bruce Lee identifies this as how he "hits without hitting."

To go against people or resist nature requires more work and effort. In many cases, it also causes more pain. If you have ever tried to force or get a child to do something they didn't want to do, you already understand what I mean.

Unfortunately, the majority of teaching practices are focused on resistance or going against people, instead of moving with them. Bruce Lee found a truth that all leaders must find: You cannot lead by resisting who people are; you must learn to accept and utilize people's natural talents to improve.

This chapter will explain how we can adjust how we teach and parent, so we can "teach without teaching." Develop without developing. This is the future model of raising children. Believe it or not, children no longer need people that "teach" them; with the worldwide internet, they have access to this in the palm of their hands. However, what a smartphone can never give them is love, true support, and specialized attention.

Teachers and Parents Must Take a Smaller Role

When looking at a teacher-student or parent-child relationship, traditional leadership models are based on influence. They identify that the teacher/parent should do most of the talking because their job is to teach. Based on this model, the more involved they are, the better the student/child will be taught.

In this chapter, I would like to introduce you to a non-traditional leadership model, which is not as popular or widely used, called No-Influence Mentoring. No-Influence Mentoring identifies the opposite: the less a teacher/parent does, the better the student/child will be taught. In fact, the teacher and parent must become "invisible" to provide the best education and development for the child.

Having been a professor I know the difficulty many people have with this model. At the university, the current model puts a professor at the top—even, in some cases, next to God! This model requires the students to adjust, go out of their way for, and praise the professor. The one person you should always "see" is the professor. You can imagine how much the other professors liked being told that they should be serving the students instead of the students serving them. This chapter will explore the logic of both the current and the future No-Influence Mentoring leadership models in greater detail.

Traditional leadership paradigm

The traditional leadership model believes that since children are young, inexperienced, and ignorant, they must be taught what to do. If left on their own, they will do the "wrong" thing—or in other words, they won't develop properly. This is not to mean they will do something "bad"; it only means they won't do what's best or most efficient.

With this paradigm, you must make some assumptions:
1. Teachers/parents know "all" important information (or everything that's best for the child).
2. The student/child will listen to the parent.
3. The student/child will be able to understand the parent.

At first, this seems like a logical paradigm. Teachers/Parents have more information and they should be able to explain to students/children. However, many people cannot see the long-term impact of this kind of model.

The impact is actually very simple. The more adults talk, the less often children do things on their own. The less the children do, the less capable they are. The less capable they are, the more mistakes they will make. The more mistakes they make, the more insecure the child will be.

This is why when the child grows up, they will need to be told what to do— it makes them feel more secure since that is how they were raised—they then are not capable of doing things on their own, making them a reactive person or a follower.

Let's put this model in a different perspective. Figure 3.1 shows a child and the course they would take if no one tried to "teach" them or change them.

Figure 3.1: A child's natural path

When an adult comes in to "teach" the child, then you now have a different path for the child (see Figure 3.2).

There is a gap between the path the parent/teacher gives the child and the path the child will naturally go down. This gap is what the business professionals call "risk," which is anything that strays away from the plan.

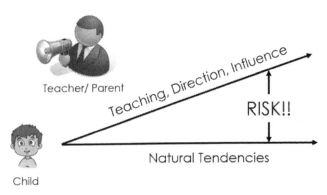

Figure 3.2: Adults tyring to change natural tendencies

Anything that differs from a child's natural tendencies will cause the child to:
1. Feel less comfortable since it is not normal to the child.
2. Feel insecure. Since it is not natural, the child will not be the best at it and is more likely to feel inadequate.
3. Fear failure. The child will believe that they are not supposed to make mistakes in life. The new path is the "perfect" path in their life, devised by adults with more experience and understanding. Thus, every time they deviate from that path, they are making a mistake and will no longer have the "perfect" life.
4. Become reactive. Since the child doesn't want to make mistakes and the new path is one they don't understand, they will not do anything unless they are told.

The farther the gap is between the child's natural tendencies, the more "risk" the child will have or the more they will be uncomfortable, feel like a failure, fear making a mistake, and not do anything unless they are told.

The following characteristics go along with a traditional teaching environment:
1. More teaching
2. More noise
3. Complexity
4. Expectations
5. Punishment
6. Resistance
7. Decision making
8. Risk
9. Stress
10. Worry / Insecurity
11. Less productive
12. More emotional
13. Less capable
14. More fear
15. Reactive
16. More resources
17. More mistakes
18. Less efficient

The impact of this model develops characteristics in a child that are not conducive to their success and happiness. Would you hire someone with these characteristics?

No-Influence mentoring

No-Influence mentoring is the opposite of the traditional leadership paradigm. It proposes that the child is perfect just the way they are, they will be okay without being told what to do, and the parent/teacher is only needed to love the child, support them, and be there for them when the child decides they need help.

This paradigm comes with some assumptions as well:
1. The adult does *not* know everything. They could be wrong.
2. The child might not be capable of understanding what the adult knows (i.e. might be best for the child to learn on their own).
3. The role of the adult is to just support and love the child.

Contrary to the traditional leadership model, this one is counterintuitive. However, when you look at the impact it will have on a child, the benefits are undeniable. With this model, the adult permits the child to do more. The more a child does, the more capable they will be. The more capable they are, the fewer mistakes they will make, and the more they will understand. Now that the child doesn't receive as much direction, they will be more secure taking the lead on things in their life.

People don't realize that confidence and capability only come with practice. A child will never feel comfortable with who they are unless they are allowed to practice being themselves. This is the danger of expectations, which attempt to control a child, forcing the child to try to be something different, which doesn't allow them to practice being themselves.

In one of my lessons, I show students a list of famous people who are very unique. In fact, these are the kind of famous people that make you think, "Who would like this person? Why does anyone like them?" Many famous people are what we call "weird," but because they have practiced being themselves for so long, they are so good at their "weirdness" that it is actually enjoyable watching them. They are funny, entertaining, or unique (Janis Joplin, Mitch Hedberg, Andy Kaufman, Ben Stein, Marilyn Manson, etc.).

Amazingly, letting a child take the path they are naturally inclined to take, enables the child to progress and develop leadership characteristics quicker than trying to get the child to take another path. This path teaches the child the following lessons:
1. The less we resist our natural tendencies, the easier life is. Their natural path is the easiest path.
2. Life is enjoyable. The path they naturally are good at will always be the most enjoyable.
3. It is okay to be different. They just need time to practice being themselves. The more they practice being themselves, the more others will see their value.

4. It is okay to make "mistakes" in life. Their natural path will lead them to make mistakes, but they will make them when they are young and the impact on their life will be minimal. In fact, because they are following their path, they will realize that there really are no "mistakes."
5. It's good to practice responsibility over one's own life at a young age because it will teach children how to minimize risk in their lives.
6. Someone who does something that comes naturally to them enjoys it, has no fear, minimizes risk, and produces more than someone who has the opposite characteristics.

When a parent/teacher minimizes their involvement and lets the child be who they naturally are, the impact is amazing. It is how leaders are developed. Many studies have shown this. One blogger cites a few different articles in her post, "*What Do Rich Parents Do That Poor Parents Don't.*"[2] She identified the main thing rich parents do is let their children be who they are. They are less involved. They are less worried about school and more worried that the child has the resources to do what they want. These parents:
1. Are less concerned about online safety
2. Don't focus on well-roundedness
3. Don't focus on academics in the summer but do give them more access to resources.
4. Don't focus on homework.
5. Don't run their lives around school calendars.

The article identified that "The more money a parent has, the less intense they are" (New York Magazine School Consultant).

Leadership is Alignment

Marcus Buckingham and Curt Coffman were leaders in the Gallup Organization—the world leader in the measurement and analysis of human attitudes, opinions, and behaviors—

for many years. Buckingham and Coffman (1999) in their book *Break All the Rules*, which was based on in-depth interviews of over 80,000 managers in over 400 companies, found that the greatest managers believe people do not change much.

> "If you hate meeting new people, can you learn to love ice-breaking with strangers? If you shy away from confrontation, can you be made to revel in the cut and thrust of debate? Can you carve new talents? Many managers and many companies assume that the answer to these questions is 'Yes' . . . The world's great managers don't share this perspective. Remember their mantra: People don't change that much. Don't waste time trying to put in what was left out. Try to draw out what was left in. That is hard enough."

Buckingham and Coffman go on to explain, "Selecting for talent is the manager's first and most important responsibility. If he/she fails to find people with the talents that are needed, then everything else he/she does to help them grow will be as wasted as sunshine on barren ground." They identified that the most successful leaders identified what people were good at and put them in the right slot with the right resources to enable them to be successful instead of trying to change people. This is what it means to be a leader. It is very different than the traditional thoughts on leadership, but this has always been understood by great leaders.

W. Edwards Deming (1982) is one of the most respected experts in the area of continuous improvement. His philosophy is the reason for the success of many manufacturers and companies, including Toyota, Apple, Pixar, and many others. Deming advised that slogans, standards, management, and control had no influence over an individual's performance. He suggested that productivity is a result of creating a system that aligns people with their strengths. Deming explains, "The leader also has responsibility to improve the system—i.e., to make it possible, on a continuing basis, for everybody to do a better job with greater satisfaction."[3] He states, "The company hired him for this job; hence has a moral obligation to put him into the right job."

Like leaders in a company, teachers and parents have an obligation to put children in the right environment for them to excel and become successful in life. So many times, we tend to tell the children to change to fit the environment, but it should be the opposite way around. Leaders, due to their greater experience and understanding, should help children by creating and finding the right environment to enable them to learn at their own level. This is called alignment. This is the main job of a parent or teacher.

When a child is young, this makes a lot of sense, but as they get older, we forget. For example, when an infant is crying, we don't tell the infant to stop or tell it to "Grow up!" Instead, we figure out the reason the baby is crying, then we try to feed it or change its diaper.

The role of the adult is to understand the child and then provide the right resources and environment to enable the child to succeed. This doesn't change as the child grows; it is the same when a student is failing chemistry or wants to look at their phone all the time. There is always a reason they are doing it. The adult's job isn't to change the child. The adult's job is to understand what is going on and provide a solution. I have found with my own child, the better the parent is at understanding the child, the less pain the child will have to go through.

Having said this, I realize how difficult it is to find the right environment for a child. I am not saying this is easy, or in some cases, even possible. What I am saying is that when a parent or teacher can do this for a child, the child flourishes and becomes more successful.

This even happens at the college level. I hired a student who was a technology expert. He was good with computers and anything dealing with electronics. There was only one issue: sometimes he wouldn't show up for work. He would disappear for a couple of days, and other times, he would come to work but look like he just woke up, didn't take a shower, and chose to wear the most wrinkled clothes he could find. Many people wanted to fire him. They felt that because he didn't follow the office rules, we should get someone else. We didn't fire him. He was a technology genius and was able to help develop all of our online courses at a time when online courses were just coming out. The key was to let him do whatever he wanted to do. If anything was time sensitive, we had to be specific on exactly what time it was needed and that it didn't matter if he did it from home, as long as it was done. We also found that by getting his cell phone number and texting him if anything was critical, he would respond quickly. He ended up doing the best work.

When people are given the ability to be themselves, it is amazing what they can do. It doesn't really matter if they do things differently than what is considered "normal."

Alignment vs. Influence

When I was in college, I had no idea "alignment" was the major job of a leader. I was taught all my life that leaders influence others. The leadership courses and trainings I took taught me a leader's actions are all focused around trying to change others. Leaders motivate, inspire, change, improve, teach, etc., all actions that influence others. This is the foundation of the traditional parent, teacher, or leadership philosophy. People assume that leaders can teach or train workers or students to improve their capability (Figure 3.3)

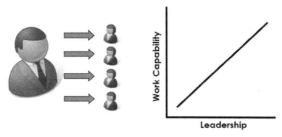

Figure 3.3: Leadership does not change work capability

Leadership is much like one of those kids' toys with different shaped blocks that only fit into specific holes (Figure 3.4). The influence leadership style is like when a child tries to shove all the shapes in one hole since it is focused on changing people. The follower's inability to change becomes the constraint. Because of the constraint, this model requires more effort and resources. It also relieves the leader from any accountability of the performance of the followers. It is the followers' fault if they don't change. This is the model that I had been taught.

At ASU, I was given an opportunity to participate in a large research effort that allowed me to study the most successful leaders and leadership philosophies. I eventually wrote my master's thesis on this topic[4]. As soon as I started this research, I came across something very disturbing: The most successful leaders did not believe in the traditional influence leadership philosophy. They believed the exact opposite, a leader doesn't influence, a leader aligns. In fact, Niccolò Machiavelli, who wrote *The Prince* (one of the oldest leadership books), identified that there is no way to influence people.

Influence Leadership

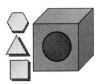

- Followers are the constraint
- Focus is changing people
- Requires lots of resources
- Relieves management from accountability

Figure 3.4: Influence tries to put a square peg in a round hole

This led me to search hundreds of articles and books to find any study, research, or empirical evidence showing that the idea of influence is correct, and I found nothing. I found no information proving the idea that one person can truly influence another person. There are many leadership philosophies and programs based on the idea of influence, but none of them have any evidence supporting the influence model. Figure 3.5 shows that the idea of influencing another person is at the root of all leadership models. Managing and motivating through training and psychology are all attempts to influence.

It goes even further. When looking at the results of programs based on the idea of influencing people, I found that almost all those programs did not work in obtaining the results they were looking for. In fact, the programs that did not focus on influencing people always had higher results than the influence programs.

My research effort entailed:
1. Reviewing over two hundred articles and books.
2. Surveying one hundred and seventy professionals on what ideas helped them more, the "influence" idea or "no-influence" idea.

After realizing there is no supporting evidence showing that a person can be influenced, I started to identify that the idea might not be right.

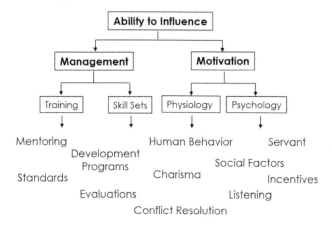

Figure 3.5: Many leadership ideas stem from influence.

I investigated more than fifteen experts in multiple industries and various fields of study (martial arts, automobile manufacturing, commercial manufacturing, self-improvement, business, management, law, and politics). These experts lived at various times throughout history: Niccolò Machiavelli, Socrates, Mozart, Mahatma Gandhi, Nelson Mandela, W. Edwards Deming, Jim Collins, Jack Welch, Bruce Lee, Soichiro Honda, Peter Drucker, James Allen, Abraham Lincoln, Rudolph Giuliani, Ricardo Semler, Marcus Buckingham, Jack Ma, and Albert Einstein.

Although all these experts do not completely agree that the idea of influence is incorrect, all their success came from ideas opposite of influence, or what I call alignment. These experts came to believe in the principles of alignment through the following:
1. Statistical Analysis (W. Edwards Deming).
2. Study of the most successful organizations (Jim Collins).
3. Study of historical precedence and results of other countries (Niccolò Machiavelli).

4. Abnormal success and advances in a specific field of study (Bruce Lee, Jack Welch, Soichiro Honda, Mahatma Gandhi, Mozart, Nelson Mandela, Peter Drucker, and James Allen).
5. In-depth interviews of eighty thousand managers (Buckingham and Coffman).
6. Followers' approval ratings (Lincoln and Giuliani).
7. Philosophy and deductive reasoning (Socrates).
8. Physics (Einstein).

When utilizing the expertise of people who have proven themselves to be experts in the past, the idea of influence starts to lose credibility and increasingly looks like the idea could be inaccurate.

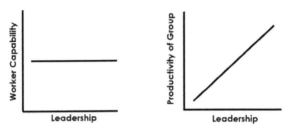

Figure 3.6: Leadership doesn't change capability, but it does change overall productivity

This led me to the "no-influence" or alignment leadership model. This model identified that no matter how much leadership you have, the worker capability level stays the same (see Figure 3.6). The leader can't impact the follower's capability. However, the greater the leadership, the greater the productivity of the entire group because when people are aligned correctly, they can perform better and do more. Going back to the child's shape toy example, the leader's main goal is to adjust the box so each person can fit into a hole that is designed for them (see Figure 3.7).

The leader is supposed to create an environment that aligns every individual according to their strengths. Of course, this is more difficult because it requires more understanding. This forces the leader to be accountable for the success of the people and the group.

No-Influence Leadership

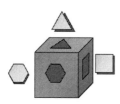

- Alignment
- Requires understanding
- Leader is constraint
- Focus is changing the system
- Efficiency

Figure 3.7: No-Influence Leadership aligns people where they fit

Here's a simple example: imagine a construction team that has two workers, one worker has a natural talent for painting and the other has a natural talent for concrete work. The two scenarios in Figure 3.8 depict the difference between the traditional (influence) leadership model and the no-influence leadership model.

Scenario 1: The influence model does not differentiate the workers; it would allow the painting expert to perform the concrete work and the concrete expert to perform the painting work. Since the workers do not know how to perform the tasks, this forces the workers to go through numerous training courses, the organization will have to supervise their work to make sure it is done properly, and the finished work will always have to be inspected to ensure quality performance.

Scenario 2: The no-influence model would first identify each individual, then it would align the workers' talents with the correct job functions; thus, the painting expert would perform the painting work and the concrete expert would perform the concrete work. Since each worker is an expert at their task, there would be a minimal need for training, supervisors, or inspections. Through aligning workers with their natural ability, it allows the organization to minimize unneeded management and training and increases the quality of their work.

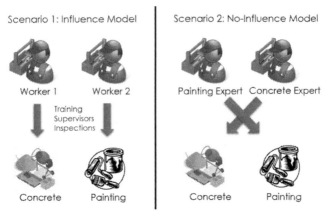

Figure 3.8: Application of No-Influence Leadership

This is much like working with children. The traditional teaching model is like scenario 1. It doesn't differentiate between children. It doesn't matter who the child is; we make each student do the same thing. Then we have to manage, train, and monitor them to make sure they don't cheat and test them to ensure they learn things correctly. The only children that really learn and excel are the ones that are built for the environment.

Scenario 2 makes more sense. It enables all children to do what they naturally do best. It allows us to minimize our teaching, monitoring, and testing and allows each student to excel.

Switching from influence to alignment causes us to focus more on changing the *system* instead of changing the *child*. It forces the leader to be more understanding and observant. It removes expectations from the child. Above all else, it requires fewer resources when performed properly.

This has been known in business for a long time but has taken many years for the industry to take a hold of the idea. Now many companies realize this is the only way to ensure they will be relevant in the future.

One company that helps us understand how this model works is Honda, the Japanese car manufacturer. They have been implementing a no-influence model for a long time. Honda's philosophy is best represented by a department head in the Honda American Manufacturing plant who "doesn't believe it's possible for managers to control employees. It's the associates who have the control, and for them to do their best work they must fully understand their jobs and give their full commitment"[5].

The way Honda both attracts and filters out individuals is through its "no-influence" attitude and environment. It is an atmosphere of accountability, taking the initiative and freedom. Honda promotes creativity and encourages employees to try new things to improve the system. However, the organization also holds people accountable to think their ideas through and utilize as many resources as they need to prevent any mishaps from occurring. As a Honda manager describes, "The system promotes efficiency because it forces people to find and solve problems early so that disturbances are avoided altogether"[6]. Very few rules and little direction are given in the Honda organization. They expect all new employees to be able to adjust quickly to this philosophy.

Honda's history shows that many individuals found that they did not feel comfortable in such a system and eventually left. The following is an account of one engineer entering the Honda culture, "Our managers expected us to know what we were supposed to do and then to assume the responsibility. Of course, now I know they left it broad on purpose. That's the way Honda does it. But in the meantime, it was very frustrating and one of the guys in the group couldn't hack it and resigned. He needed a job description and was lost without one. It's been two years, and I and the others are doing quite well"[7]. The no-influence model didn't work for some people as they weren't raised with it and had a hard time adjusting to it. This is why we should start using this model with our students while in their youth to help prepare them.

Honda realizes that if someone is aligned in a position that suits them, they won't have to be told what to do, they will already know what to do. Thus, in their culture, they filter employees out by allowing the employees to identify where they best fit. Giving the employees the freedom to make their own job, doing what they know how to do. And if they don't know what to do and they don't feel comfortable anywhere, then to let them go to another company.

This is evidence to support using a no-influence model when children are young. As they grow up and are required to be leaders in organizations, they will already be used to this way of doing things.

Releasing Control

The hardest part of being a leader is learning to accept life for what it is and people for who they are. Influence has convinced people that when they do not agree with life or people, they should exert their control over them and influence/change it or them. Influence has taught people that the solution is to resist, control, and change. This mindset of control and influence is what brings the expectations on children. They are not smart enough; they don't have enough self-control; they don't care enough; they are too dirty, etc.

As we started this chapter with Bruce Lee, we will end it with Bruce Lee. He agreed with the no-influence leadership philosophy, believing that trying to change life and people from their natural tendencies will decrease success and efficiency.

Bruce Lee followed three main principles that helped him to release control:
1. Wu-Wei
2. Law of Harmony
3. Law of No-Interference

Wu-Wei

The word Naturalism is derived from the Chinese phrase Wu-Wei, which is defined as non-action (Wu meaning no and Wei meaning action). The theory being that top performance is reached when the mind is not controlled (when no action is taken against the mind) but is allowed to react naturally. It is like a pitcher catching a ball hit directly at him. The ball is approaching too fast for the pitcher to tell his mind to lift his hand and catch the ball; instead, at that moment, he releases control of his mind and allows it to react on its own. When control is released, it quickens the pitcher's reaction and increases his accuracy in catching the ball. Bruce Lee practiced trying to release control of himself to enable himself to perform better. This also helped him to minimize trying to control others. The more a leader releases control of his organization, the quicker and more efficient it will be[8].

Law of harmony

The law of harmony is another main principle Bruce Lee taught. "The law of harmony, in which one should be in harmony with, and not in opposition to, the strength and force of the opposition. This means that one should do nothing that is not natural or spontaneous; the important thing is not to strain in any way"[9]. The law of harmony shows adults a new way to deal with children—a way that does not oppose children but supports them. This new way should enable the teacher not to strain but to minimize stress and effort.

Law of Non-Interference

The law of non-interference is a basic principle of Taoism: "That one should be in harmony with, not rebellion against, the fundamental laws of the universe. Preserve yourself by following the natural bend of things and don't interfere. Remember, never to assert yourself against nature; never be in frontal opposition to any problems, but to control it by swinging with it"[10]. This is the basis for Bruce Lee's fighting style as mentioned at the beginning of the chapter. He teaches that it is futile to try to interfere with another individual's natural actions. Instead, one must flow with the action. This is just as true in the realm of martial arts as it is in business or education.

To try to change an individual's natural behavior takes a great amount of energy and resources; it is inefficient. In order to maximize an individual's capability, it is important to align a person in a position where that person's natural behaviors can produce the desired results.

Thus, he teaches that the wise master will always mold his ways to fit the ignorant, and the ignorant will try to control everything to fit their own style. This is a fundamental change that the principle of no-influence brings to the current conception of leadership and is the main message of this chapter. For adults to become leaders and mentors, they must learn to not interfere with a child's development, but instead they must adjust to the child's needs and create an environment that allows the child to follow their natural course.

With this philosophy, even if a child does not want to learn, the adult's role is to find the right situation for the child to develop. As Bruce Lee directs when facing opposition, "Cooperate with your opponent. Do not resist or interrupt his flow of movement. Instead of stopping his force, complete it by following him... Remember this—what you will do depends on your opponent; that is why we say—be the complement and not the opposite of the opponent's force,"[11]

What is the Purpose of Teaching?

When a teacher first learns about the No-Influence Mentoring method, they first ask, "How does a teacher not have an influence on their students?" I explain it this way:

Influence denotes that the teacher has somehow impacted the student by giving them knowledge or understanding that they would not have received otherwise. This would mean the teacher controls the amount of information the child receives. However, we know this is inaccurate because a teacher has never been able to ensure that all students comprehended the same amount of information at the end of the class. This means that the teacher doesn't determine how much the student learns, the student does. Teachers can only share information, and students will learn what they are willing to receive.

The next question a teacher will usually ask is "What is the purpose of teaching if influence doesn't exist?" Most teachers use the words "teaching" and "influencing" synonymously. People can't picture teaching without influence. When a teacher realizes that they don't have influence, they are more likely to:
1. Minimize the amount of information they teach.
2. Accurately identify who the students are and what they are capable of learning.
3. Conform their lessons to the students' capabilities.

As Bruce Lee stated, "I am not teaching you anything. I just help you to explore yourself."[12]

No-Influence mentoring changes the leader's role from trying to teach, train, and lead to:
1. Identifying individuals.
2. Alignment of resources.
3. Creating an environment that helps the students.

The many definitions of teaching all identify teaching as helping another person to acquire knowledge or understanding. This is a correct definition, but it never identifies that the teacher is imparting this knowledge and understanding; it is just saying the teacher is helping the child to obtain it. It could be that the teacher does this by providing the right environment for the child to learn it on their own.

The No-Influence Mentoring model is the first model that doesn't try to change children. It changes the role of the parent, mentor, and teacher to be one that loves, supports, and uses their resources to help a student along their natural path in life. Amazingly, the data shows that children are more successful when they are loved, supported, and feel comfortable with who they are.

Chapter Summary and Goals

You can begin to adjust your teaching/parenting/mentoring style in many ways. However, all of them come down to this simple non-action: do less. It is amazing how you can improve your teaching/mentoring more by simply decreasing your action. It is a true win-win situation.
In the next chapters, we will discuss specific actions you can take to move to this style of mentoring. But to practice and begin down that path, you can try:

1. Focusing on saying less every time you talk with people (other adults as well as children).

2. Tracking how many times you try to "change" people around you. This could be their actions or their opinions. Then assess how much you currently try to change people.
3. Pick a person in your life that you try to influence the most. It could be you get in a lot of arguments with them or that you just try to change them because you care a lot about them. When you pick the person, practice not telling them anything this week. Instead of trying to *teach* them or influence them, you will now just try to support them and help them with whatever they need.
4. Every time you get into a conversation, ask, "What should the purpose of this conversation be, if I am not trying to influence this person?"

By trying any one of these activities, it will either make you more aware of how much we, in general, try to influence others or it will help you to minimize wasted energy on changing people and instead help you to align people in your life to help you become more productive. For more activities, visit my free course at LeadAZ.org/NIM

---

[1] TIME, *TIME 100 Persons of The Century*, (TIME Magazine, 1999).
[2] Trunk, P. (2013). "What Rich Parents Do That Poor Parents Don't". [...PT...]. https://education.penelopetrunk.com/2013/12/02/what-do-rich-parents-do-that-poor-parents-dont/
[3] W. Edwards Deming, *Out of the Crisis*, (The MIT Press, 2000), 213
[4] Jacob Kashiwagi, *Leadership is Alignment Not Influence*, (Arizona State University, Tempe, AZ, 2007)
[5] Robert L. Shook, *Honda: An American Success Story*, (Prentice Hall Direct, 1988)
[6] Ibid.
[7] Ibid.
[8] Caldwell, L. *Bruce Lee: The Artist of Life*, (Tuttle Publishing, Boston, MA, 2001)
[9] Bruce Lee, *Bruce Lee Striking Thoughts: Bruce Lee's Wisdom for Daily Living*, (Tuttle Publishing, 2015)
[10] Ibid.

[11] Bruce Lee, *Chinese Gung Fu: The Philosophical Art of Self Defense*, (Twentieth Printing, 2005)
[12] Attributed to Bruce Lee, original source unknown.

4
No-Influence Mentoring

Introduction

In the previous chapter, we identified that teachers and parents should minimize their importance, and thus, do less and exert less control over the child or student. This is a difficult thing to do. In fact, sometimes we might not even realize how much we are doing or how much we are trying to control others. While I was working in a research group at ASU, I went through an experience that helped me understand this.

During a particularly stressful time, when there were multiple deadlines approaching, I was complaining to my mentor, who happened to be my father, that I was too busy. I had been working over sixty hours a week and it was too much for me. My father gave me some advice that I always remembered. He said, "The reason you are stressed and have so many issues is because you are trying to take accountability for responsibilities that are not yours." He then explained to me that many of my tasks were not my responsibility; they should be assigned to other staff members. In fact, many of the tasks couldn't get done without the other people anyway.

I learned that a leader is not someone that takes other people's responsibilities and does everything themselves. If you do everything yourself, you don't need anyone else. As we discussed in the previous chapter, a leader is someone that understands people and can give the appropriate responsibilities to the right people. I also realized that one of the reasons I was trying to do more and be more controlling over the research work was that I was confused about what I was supposed to be accountable for. I was never supposed to be accountable for doing other people's work.

This is the same issue that parents and teachers experience. It is natural for us to feel responsible for a child's life and their success. We feel accountable for them. However, this mentality causes stress and unneeded conflict. Too often, parents and teachers are taking more accountability than needed and not allowing the child to take responsibility for their own self. This is very detrimental to both the adult and the child. The child grows up in an environment where they don't learn to take accountability for their life and the adult is overworked, stressed, and unhappy.

This is the main change of No-Influence Mentoring: parents and teachers are not responsible for making sure their students and children learn. Your job is *not* to teach. Your job is to support the children in your lives so they can learn and grow at their natural pace. A mentor should listen, observe, and then provide a direction to the student so they can teach themselves. Easier said than done.

No-Influence mentoring isn't just a theory. It has been developed over years of industry and classroom testing. In this chapter, you'll learn what No-Influence Mentoring looks like in practice.

The Background of No-Influence Mentoring

No-Influence mentoring was developed using the most licensed (60 licenses)[1] project delivery model at ASU (US News' most innovative university for five years in a row)[2]. The business model was called the Best Value Approach (BVA). The BVA was the only business model that had documentation on multiple projects showing that it could improve the performance and efficiency of projects.

Its performance line is as follows[3]:
- 28 years of research in the industry
- 2,000+ projects
- $6.6B total project cost
- 96 percent owner satisfaction
- 9 countries and 32 states
- 300+ published books & journal papers

The BVA was developed by Dr. Dean Kashiwagi in 1992. If you didn't guess already, Dr. Dean is my father. I went to work at ASU as a Research Professor, because I wanted to work with my father. We developed an honors course at Barrett, the Honor's College (New York Times "Gold Standard")[4], that would teach the top 10 percent of students at the university from all concentrations (over seventy-four different degree concentrations) the principles of the business model. We offered up to six sessions of the class, for up to 250 students a semester. The class became so popular that if a student didn't sign-up for the class right when registration opened at 6 a.m., they couldn't get into the class.

The education program showed impressive performance results. With a 94 percent student satisfaction rating, the course decreased reported stress by 28 percent and helped many students overcome significant life challenges (depression, substance abuse, social anxiety, etc.)[5].

In 2013, two of our Ph.D. students (Alfredo Rivera and Jake Gunnoe) identified the value of making this education available to high school students. Through ASU funded competitions, they were awarded funding to create the non-profit organization: Leadership Society of Arizona (LSA). LSA adapted the BVA education model for teenage students. The goal of the program was to help address issues of mental instability and academic deficiencies (grades, test scores, attendance, etc.).

After six years of program implementation, LSA showed staggering results:
- 17 schools, 70+ programs, 2,300+ students
- 94 percent client satisfaction rating (students, parents, and administrators)
- 85 percent of parents report significant behavioral changes in their children
- 92 percent of students feel more accountable for their success
- 67 percent of students report feeling less stressed
- 55 percent feel more confident about their futures
- 30 percent increase in GPA
- 89 percent increase in standardized test passing rate

Three Principles of No-Influence Mentoring

This model is not black and white. Everyone is somewhere in between as there is no wrong or right way to practice this approach. However, the goal is to practice no-influence as much as possible and minimize traditional control-based leadership.

This book focuses on using the principles to help children and students in the family and school; however, this can also be used to help college students and adults.

No-Influence Mentoring is made up of three main principles:

Individual centered
Each person is unique and will need to be approached differently. No two people can learn and grow in the same way. The only way to ensure they can learn the quickest is by spending time to understand who they are and what they want. The goal is to adjust all interactions to fit with what the individual needs. This means that the individual identifies the purpose of the teaching and what content they will learn. For adults mentoring children, the child should determine the structure and interaction of the mentorship.

Simplicity structured
Since complexity causes stress—one of the biggest factors that prevents people from learning and improving—the heart of all leadership is to simplify concepts. When things are too complex, it's impossible to understand and learn. So instead, everything must be simple and easy to follow. This means that the mentor must ensure that any new information provided to the child can be quickly understood and learned. This model tries to move toward teaching people

patterns and natural laws, explanations that help people understand *why* things are happening. Simple means less work, less stress, less difficulty.

Action focused

The main goal of this approach is to help the child accomplish something. One of the main characteristics of successful people is that they *did* something. The greatest way a child can "fail" is by *doing nothing*. If a child acts, especially upon something that they want to do and that they enjoy, it is hard for the child not to succeed. When a child learns to act and motivate themselves, they learn how to improve themselves. If a child learns this at a young age, they develop the skills to become successful. And like any skill, the more it is practiced, the better it becomes. This is the most important skill a child can learn while they are young: to act.

No-Influence mentoring can be adapted to any parenting or teaching style as well as any academic curriculum (e.g., math, English, history, etc.). The model doesn't focus on the *content*; it focuses on the *student*. This is the same with parenting. The more a parent changes their focus from trying to parent, to understanding the child, the better the child will be. The more that you focus on who the child is and what they want, the more the child will want to learn and the better they will do.

Conclusion

The next chapters will review each of the three No-Influence Mentoring principles and how to incorporate them into your life. The chapters will be structured as follows:
1. An explanation of the principle and the concept behind it.
2. A list of simple steps to adjust your teaching/parenting style to adhere to the principle.

Most of the actions and steps will be simple and self-explanatory; however, each chapter will also provide an in-depth explanation to help you apply the principles immediately.

Chapter Summary and Goals

Stepping back and allowing a child to take accountability for themselves is very difficult to do. I liken it to the first week my first child was born. The baby was making a noise that I was unfamiliar with, but it was annoying. It is usually known as "crying." There was a lot of it. Sometimes it was unbearable. The baby would cry for many reasons: needed to eat, had a dirty diaper, felt uncomfortable, or was in a bad mood. Often, the baby did not know what he needed to feel better. I quickly realized you can minimize the crying by figuring out what the baby needs, but you can't get rid of it. It is just a part of the baby growing.

Growth is uncomfortable and difficult for children. It is also difficult to watch someone grow. It is challenging to try to be calm and just hold the baby despite all the crying. However, this is also what is needed with older students. For parents and teachers to just be there with them, even though they are hard to understand, their actions are difficult to be around, and they don't even know what they want half the time.

To help you make your transition to No-Influence Mentoring a little easier, start by focusing on the children's responsibilities:
1. Identify what you view your responsibilities are.
2. Identify what responsibility is your child's or student's.
3. Identify how you currently divide up your responsibilities.
4. Identify ways you feel you can simplify, individualize, and help your child to learn to improve and change.

For more activities, visit my free course at LeadAZ.org/NIM

---

[1] Dean Kashiwagi, *2019 Best Value Approach Lessons Learned*, (KSM inc., Mesa, AZ 2019)
[2] US News, *Most Innovative Schools 2019*, (usnews.com, 2020)
[3] Kashiwagi, *2019 Best Value Approach Lessons Learned*
[4] Frank Bruni, *A Prudent College Path*, (New York Times, 2015)
[5] Jake Gunnoe & David Krassa, *Application of Best Value Approach to Resolve Educational Non-Performance*, (Journal for the Advancement of Performance Information and Value, Vol. 11, 2019) 82-104

5
Individual Centered

Individual Centered vs. System Centered

A leader knows that a structure is only as stable as the foundation it is built upon, which for all organizations is the individuals that make it up. Thus, the organizations that do not continually try to strengthen their individuals will eventually collapse. Organizations are starting to realize this today, putting more effort into finding ways to keep their good people and continually train and develop them. However, most organizations today are still system centered. In other words, their focus is on maintaining the system and requiring the employees to adjust to the organization's system. In such organizations, resources and people are only as important as their ability to support the system.

An individual-centered structure is focused on the individuals in an organization. The system is built to support and help the individuals in the organization. It realizes that the stronger the individuals are, the more stable and productive the organization will be. This has been proven many times. Let me tell you a story of one organization, SEMCO, a Brazilian company, that made this change. In the 1990s the son of the founder, Ricardo Semler, took over and changed the structure from system centered to individual centered. He made the following changes:

1. The employees determined what type of work they performed. If no one wanted to work on something, they stopped doing business in that area.
2. Employees determined their own pay.
3. You were hired when someone in the company was willing to work with you.
4. Everyone had access to company finances and how much everyone else got paid.
5. There was a board seat reserved for anyone in the company that wanted to vote on company business at board meetings.
6. Employees determined who would be the managers, all the way up to the CEO.

These were radical changes at the time they were performed, and many people felt there was no way a company could operate like this. How can you allow employees to do whatever they want and choose their own salary? This would be like allowing kids in a family to make their own rules and do whatever they wanted! The common thought was they will do nothing and take all the company's money. Amazingly, despite what everyone thought would happen, these changes improved the performance and the success of the company. SEMCO did so well, if you invested a couple of thousand dollars into this company forty years ago, you would be a millionaire today.

Parents and teachers must make the same changes Ricardo Semler made with his company in their families and classrooms. The transition requires moving from an environment that expects the students and children to support the system to a structure where the system supports them. The transitions will create a system that respects the children and students and focuses on what they want.

The Child-Centered Environment

Leaders know that everyone is valuable. In a company or family, removing one person from the environment will cause instability. Everyone has equal value. This equality causes a leader to treat each person with the same amount of respect for who they are. It doesn't matter their age, gender, or intelligence level. A leader doesn't discriminate.

I noticed a good example when I was spending time with my brother's family. His oldest son (who is four years old) received two shirts. He wore one, and his younger sister (two years old) wanted to wear the other. So, the mother put the shirt on her. When the son found out, he protested. He said that it was his shirt and he didn't want his sister wearing it. It was a tough dilemma for the parents, but the sister eventually won, and the son was told to let her wear it. For the next ten minutes, the son protested until the sister agreed to take it off.

Many parents and teachers have experienced a similar situation. If the son was a fifty-year-old man, the situation would have been very different. He would have been given more respect for his property. No one would force him to share. It is a big temptation when working with children to treat them as if they are second-class citizens. They are not given the same respect as adults.

In an individual-centered environment, a leader treats everyone with the same respect. Meaning, if my brother's older son didn't want the younger sister wearing the shirt, then the younger sister would not be allowed to wear the shirt. Here both opinions were respected as the parents respected their daughter's by asking the son if she could have it. Since it wasn't her property, the decision was up to the son, but her opinion was respected in the asking. Just as we do with adults, each person's opinions and decisions need to be respected. The only time this is not allowed is when a person's actions infringe on another person's health or safety. In the case of sharing, there's not always an easy solution for children, but if we don't respect them as individuals (their wants, needs, and property), they will never learn to respect themselves.

This type of treatment is a good example of when the environment is not individual centered; it is system centered. The system could be a family, class, or business, but in a system-centered environment, everything else is more important than the person. The person can only get their respect if their needs fit within the system.

Now, it is important to note here that providing a child with unlimited resources doesn't necessarily make the system individual centered. I have met many wealthy families and schools that provide many resources to their students/children, but the children are not respected or cared for. This is what many people call *a family with everything but without love in the home*.

When an environment doesn't respect the child, it teaches the child to not respect other people. It teaches them that they do not have control over their own life. It teaches them that they have to follow the system and the system controls and governs what they do. This is detrimental in all families. This is known as thinking inside the box. It teaches the child to be a follower.

INDIVIDUAL CENTERED

At first, this makes sense to most people, but then they start thinking and ask, "How can you treat a child like an adult when an adult is mature and a child is immature and doesn't have enough information to make the right choices?"

The answer is simple: in an individual-centered environment, we *respect everyone equally*, but we do not *treat everyone equally*. We treat each person based on their level of understanding and capability.

My sister explained this best to her kids when they requested equal treatment when getting Christmas gifts. She explained if you all want equal gifts, that means everyone gets the exact same thing. This means if I get your sister a princess dress, everyone will get a princess dress. This wasn't the answer they were expecting as my sister has one girl and four boys. However, she said, if you want to be treated fairly, then I will try to get the best gift for each of you, depending on what you will enjoy the most.

Leaders are very aware that no two people are equal. Due to everyone being different and having gone through different experiences in life, no two people will be the exact same or will have the exact same skill level in anything.

This mentality causes a leader to treat each person with the same amount of respect for who they are (fairly), but the leader does not treat each person the same (equally). The leader recognizes that each person wants to be treated differently depending on who they are.

For example, in my office, I respect all my employees. However, would I let all my employees borrow my car? The answer is definitely no! Some of them do not drive well, and the likelihood of them getting into an accident or causing damage to the car is high. This is the same with most things with my coworkers. I don't discuss the same things with all of them. To some, I talk about raising kids, and to others, I talk about their relationship with their spouse. It just depends on if they have kids or if they are newly married.

In an individual-centered environment, it is the same. Just because you respect each person and will be kind and understanding and supportive of everyone, doesn't mean you treat them the same or talk to everyone about the same things. I would let some employees work from home every day if they wanted to, and some I would always make them come to work. This is not because I like them more or less, this is because I treat them based upon who they are. Some will work better when they consistently have to come into work.

Some children are more mature than others, some are more capable, some understand certain things in life more than others. Thus, depending on their capability, you should determine individually what you allow them to do, have access to, or talk with them about.

The following characteristics follow an individual-centered environment:
1. The purpose of the family/organization is to *help* the individual.
2. The organization/family is helping the student or child achieve what they want in life, not what someone else thinks they should want.
3. The individual is respected and treated fairly.
4. The individual has input on how the family/classroom is run.

5. The education that is taught is at the level of the individual and is being taught in a way that will best help the individual to progress.

Each person will have a different level of comfort in applying this **principle**. I encourage each teacher and parent to do what they feel comfortable doing. If this is a big change from how you usually approach your students/children, then start slow. Identify one thing you can do from the steps outlined in the rest of this section to move toward this way of treating people and see how it goes. Then gradually make more changes according to what you feel comfortable with.

Creating an individual-centered environment is not an easy thing to do. While the concept is simple, applying it is very difficult for most people, especially in a family or classroom with more children or students.

Steps to shaping teaching and parenting around the student:
1. Identify who the individual is.
2. Identify what the individual wants.
3. Enable the individual to shape the class or family.
4. Reduce direction and rules.

1. Identifying Who the Individual Is

The most critical part of being able to create an individual-centered environment is understanding who the individual is. This means that if you are teaching an English class, while you need to know the English level of your students, you also need to know everything about these students. And not just one student, but all of your students. This becomes difficult in a public classroom setting when a teacher typically will have thirty kids and around six class periods, which means each year they could have 180 students.

During my time at ASU, sometimes I would have up to 250 students a semester. I used several techniques to get to know my students:

1. The very first assignment I gave was a profile sheet on themselves. I formatted the sheet so it was easy for me to quickly review their information. This enabled me to get important information on each student before I met them in person.
2. I conducted ten- to fifteen-minute interviews at the start of the semester. This took time, but in that small amount of time, I formed a bond with many of my students.
3. During the semester, I added questions to test and quizzes to gauge how the students felt about the class and their personal lives.
4. I asked them to fill out an end of the semester survey that gave me feedback on what they learned and what was valuable to them. I would use this to adjust curriculum and class management.

During the semester, I made it a point to talk to different students each class period. As I learned more about the students, I updated their biographies so I wouldn't forget. By the end of the semester, I knew most of the students very well and became familiar with details about their lives and their struggles.

To make this process easier, I tracked all student information on a spreadsheet small enough to fit on one sheet of paper. This enabled me to quickly identify the students that needed more attention (if you would like to see some example spreadsheets, email me at Team@LeadAZ.org)

INDIVIDUAL CENTERED

If you are a parent, this step will be a lot easier as you see your children almost every day and you usually have less than 180 of them. You also have known them for their entire lives. However, even though parents work with smaller groups of individuals and spend more time with them, it does not mean that the parents really know who their children are. In fact, because of parental expectations, you might have an even harder time recognizing who your child *really* is.

If you're a parent and you want to get to know your children, you should do the same thing a teacher does for their students. Spend time doing activities with your children and making sure you spend time interviewing or talking with them about how their life is going. This is the only way to understand and meet their needs.

How you document and get feedback from your children might be a little less formal, but it is still important. In fact, for parents, it is even more important that you are continually following up with your children since you are the only "sane" adult that can speak with them one-on-one every day.

Sometimes, it's very difficult to talk to students or children. Many kids don't like talking. As you practice more and more, it will become less difficult because the children will realize you do not have any expectations of them. As they realize you want to help them and make them happy, they will be more willing to open up.

Many parents worry because their child doesn't like talking, but this is very normal for many children I've seen. Sometimes it requires new activities or new environments. Sometimes it requires changing a rule or expectation that is causing a lot of stress. One summer, I had a thirteen-year-old student who refused to talk to anyone. I told him that it was okay if he didn't want to participate in class—he could sit and relax. Later, I started talking to him about video games, and that's when he finally opened up. That was the beginning of a long and fruitful friendship with that student.

For more tips on how to start unique conversations with kids, I would recommend reading Jed Jurchenko's book, *131 Conversations that Engage Kids*.

2. Identifying What the Individual Wants

Once you have a good grasp on who your children or students are, then you can begin to figure out what they want. It is important to remember that most children and teenagers don't even know what they want. Even worse, many times they think they know what they want, but they really don't. This means that if you ask them, they may unknowingly give you an untrue answer. It may sound confusing that a child will tell you they want something even if they don't really want it, but this happens all the time.

Younger children may say that all they want is candy and soda for dinner, but if they only eat junk food, then their health would suffer. These children don't realize that candy and soda won't make them happy in the long run as it will keep them from playing outside and having fun. The same with older kids—they might think that all they want to do is get on their phones, but they don't realize the negative effects that it might have on their mental health.

In an individual-centered environment, you can deal with a child or student that wants to do something detrimental to them (like only eating junk food) in several ways. I will remind you, the main goal of the individual-centered environment and No-Influence Mentoring is, as much as you can, to not *force* your child to do something. You want them to take accountability for their own life. Emphasis on **as much as you can**. There are varying degrees of this and depending on the capability and intelligence of your child, you might not be able to do this "perfectly." In some cases, because you feel your child is in danger, you will need to step in and "control" or "force" them to do something. However, the object is to minimize this. I recommend taking these actions when a child wants to do something detrimental:

1. Let them do what they want until you feel they will hurt themselves. Eating only candy for a couple of days won't hurt anyone. Many times, children will figure out it isn't the best when they can put it to the test.
2. Talk with them and work to figure out a compromise that they are willing to do.
3. Provide them with additional information, which may change their mind on what they want to do.
4. Try to adjust something to create a win-win situation. For example, if they only want junk food, maybe they just haven't tried the *right* healthy food yet, or maybe they haven't tried the healthy food in the right way, or maybe if they know they can have some junk food with each meal, then they would be fine eating healthier food. There are a million ways to adjust something to align your desire with theirs.

Here are some tips to remember when dealing with children:
1. **What they want at one point in their life might not be what they want at another point. What they want at the beginning of the semester might change by the end of the semester.**
   (In fact, you should hope this happens, as it shows they learned something or understand themselves better.)
2. **If children want something, they do it.**
   (Regardless of what they say, if the child is willing to do it, you know they want it to some degree.)
3. **If children don't want something, they won't do it.** (Again, don't listen to what they say; many might say they want something, but if they don't do it, you know they don't really want it.)
4. **Children probably don't want the same things as you.**
   (Children don't see the same way as adults. Even if they are doing something, it is probably for a different reason than you think, so it is important that you really listen and try to understand from the point of view of the child.)
5. **It takes time for children to figure out what they want.**
   (Be patient; it is tough to figure out what you want when you have so little information and experience in life.)

The purpose of finding out what the individual wants is that people will always perform better when they are doing what they want. Aligning what the students want with your class or your goal as a family will set them up for success.

For example, when I was mentoring a high school student, we asked him what he wanted. The first thing he could think of was playing basketball. After setting some goals for him to improve his basketball skills, we quickly found out he really didn't care about basketball. Why? Because he never accomplished his goal of improving and never practiced.

We talked to him for a few weeks, suggested new ideas, asked him unique questions, and soon found out what he really cared about was getting a job.

How did we know? Once we set a goal to get a job, he sent us a draft resume in three days. His attitude quickly turned around for each call we had with him. However, this was short-lived as his parents eventually told him he couldn't get a job. This was unfortunate, but even though we couldn't help him find a job anymore, he realized we were trying to help him with what he wanted, and he continued to talk with us. Amazingly, eventually his parents did allow him to find a job, and he didn't need any motivation from me to get him to find one. He started looking right away by himself.

When you want to find out what a child wants, follow the same simple steps:
1. Ask them.
2. Encourage action.
3. Pay attention to how they react over the course of a week.
4. Talk to them about their choice.
5. Suggest new ideas or strategies.
6. Repeat the process.

3. Enable the Individual to Shape the Class or Family

As a leader, anytime you can give your students or children the ability to determine what, when, where, or how, you enable them to take more accountability for what they are doing and encourage them to take more of a leadership role themselves. The more students or children you have, the tougher this is. However, you can do this with a group of children.

The previous steps will help you greatly in trying to do this one. To involve students more, you can:

1. Be transparent with the students/children. Let them know your constraints and what your goals and objectives are. The more you include them, the more you will see them naturally participate in decision making. It is important to remember that you are still talking with children. So, you need to try to relay things as simply as you can. The more you talk to children like adults, the more emotionally stable they will become.

2. Ask them their opinion when you don't know. When you reach out to them, children will be really honest with you about what they think and what they see. However, make sure you listen when they speak because children also are very aware when someone is just asking and not really listening. When they see insincerity, they will shut down and stop talking. It might take some time for them to gain confidence that you will listen if in the past they have felt fear in being honest. Also, remember that children might not even know what to think or how they feel about something. Being able to explain yourself is a talent. You might need to help your student or child learn to explain what they think. We take for granted having an opinion sometimes; it is something we developed over years.

3. Give them options. When left to figure things out for themselves, students have a tough time deciding what they should do. A steppingstone to that is giving them two options to choose from. Letting them pick empowers them. Remember not to give too many options or it overwhelms them, though.

4. Reducing Direction and Rules

In a system-focused environment, one keeps order through directions and rules for people to follow. In an individual-centered environment, we want the individual to determine their own direction instead of someone external telling the individual what to do. At first, this will seem like a more difficult task than the traditional direction and rules system. However, in the long run, it will not only be more effective, but it will also enable the family, classroom, or organization to be more productive.

While direction and rules can fit into the individual-centered environment, they must be focused on the individual. Here's what this might look like (depending on your student or child, some of these will work better, no need to implement all of them):

1. The individual develops their own rules. In a family, this means that the parents will work with the children to determine a set of rules that the family will follow. (This applies to school-aged children as that is the focus of our book. Younger children don't need "rules" per se as much as they just need you to create an environment that enables them to live without hurting themselves and without constraining them.)
2. The individual agrees to follow the rules of their own free will and choice. The key here is that the individual agrees to follow the provided rules whether or not they helped to develop them. If an individual sees a rule or direction as something that will benefit them, they will agree to follow it. It then becomes an internal choice rather than an external requirement.

3. The individual seeks direction and guidance. When an individual wants help and is ready to listen to others, they will ask. This is the only time that parents can offer information to a child and it will benefit them. Leaders can create a structure that makes it easier for the individual to seek and ask for help and advice, but in the end, the individual must be the one to initiate it.
4. The individual's behavior is a safety risk or causes the leader too much stress. When a child doesn't understand a rule, it might be best for their safety to enforce the rule. Other times, parents or teachers need to enforce a rule to help with their own stress and wellbeing.

In an individual-centered environment, we want to minimize any requirement on the individual that doesn't come from the individual. This means trying to minimize any rule that is not needed for the stability of the family or organization. Ideally, rules should be tailored to each individual, but sometimes a family rule is required.

If you have a rule that is not being followed or you have to expend a lot of energy to enforce it, you probably need to change the rule. Obviously, your rule is not working as it is not something your students or children can actually follow. It is too much for them. Usually if you adjust the rule to something they will agree with or can actually follow, it will not only be more beneficial for them but it will also be adhered to. In my family, sometimes it was about giving the right chore to the right child. Or sometimes it was just lowering the expectation.

INDIVIDUAL CENTERED

Shaping a class/family around the child/student means creating a structure that is possible for them to do well in. For example, let's say a teacher has a rule that homework needs to be turned in on the due date or the student gets no credit. There are two scenarios for this:

Scenario 1—All students are getting their homework turned in on time and are happy with the rule.

Scenario 2—20 percent of the students are not getting their homework turned in on time and are not happy with this rule.

If it is scenario 1, then this is a good rule. It is helping the students and it is something that they can work with. If it is scenario 2, then this is not a good rule and needs to be changed. The goal is to adjust it so all students can do well. This could mean allowing students to turn the homework in late without a penalty; it could mean having a penalty for the late work.

This is much the same for a parent dealing with children in a family. The goal is to shape the family so that each child is able to do well in the family. Below, I've included some of my family's journal entries when I was growing up; it's a good example of when a rule is not working:
- 3/25/1984—Child 1 is grounded for two weeks from everything for lying.
- 5/13/1984—Child 1 kicked Child 2 [foster child] and is grounded for one week.
- 8/19/1984—Boys being naughty to mom / spank harder.
- 1/12/1986—Child 1 threw away some homework papers and lied to mom. Is grounded from karate for one month.

- 1/26/1986—Child 1 continues to be a challenge to his mother. He also continues to do less than his capabilities. Child 1 lied to his teacher: 4 more weeks of 2 bathrooms, Fri, Sat, Sun. Child 1 will do dishes, grounded from riding bikes and skates, no TV for 6 more weeks.

The journal entries show that the rules were punishing my brother. I remember that my brother was always grounded when I was younger. He basically couldn't do anything when he was a child. The question is: Does this work? In my brother's case, it didn't. If you look down at the bottom two entries, those are two years later than the first three. You can tell that the punishments weren't working because he was doing things that were more serious than the two years before. The "spank harder" approach obviously was not the best solution in my family's case. The amazing thing is that my parents did learn, and they changed.

I come from a family of eight kids. I am the fourth child, which puts me as the youngest of the first four kids and the oldest of the last four kids. Right in the middle of everyone. As my older siblings grew up and I turned twelve, a unique thing happened in my family. My parents decided to change our family from a system-centered family to an individual-centered family. In doing this, they ended up performing a crazy experiment with my younger siblings. They started by asking "What happens if you focus on supporting the child in what they want rather than telling them what to do?" This question led them to eliminate all rules unless they came from the child. This was a drastic shift in the normal operations of the family. Both my mom and dad are Japanese, our heritage is based on a very strict rule-oriented environment where you always listen to your elders. Up until that point, we had rules determining everything, such as when to go to bed and wake up, when to eat, when we could watch television, when we could play with friends, what we could do on certain days of the week, what we had to participate in, instruments we had to play, what grades we needed to get in school, etc.

At first, the experiment didn't seem to work. My two youngest brothers got in the most trouble, caused my parents the most consternation, and were growing up to be "good-for-nothing rotten brats". My youngest brother was the only one to get involved with the police for sneaking on the elementary school's roof at night. My two youngest brothers never helped around the house, were always playing video games, and did not really excel at school at all. In fact, many times they would skip school.

That last paragraph may cause some stress—you may doubt your ability to endure that kind of behavior. First, not all children will be this "bad"; you can see how tough my parents had it. Second, I share this example because my parents went to the extreme with the model and released all control: had no rules, no punishments, and supported my brothers no matter what they wanted to do. You might not want to go to this extreme. And lastly, this was tough, but if you met my two younger brothers today, you would see the sacrifice was worth it.

So yeah while it was rough going for a while, as they got older, something happened. It seemed that their freedom and the support that they received from the family to allow them to be who they were somehow helped them mature faster than most kids. By the time they were juniors and seniors in high school, they began making decisions in their life that helped them become more responsible, helpful, intelligent, and proactive. I was working at ASU at the time, and I would trust my brothers more than some of my college graduate students. From my perspective at the end of this experiment, my youngest brothers became smarter, more innovative, mature, and service oriented than all of us. It was an amazing thing to watch.

Conclusion

The last way to implement a student-centered environment is by doing the following:
1. Identify everything you expect a student or child to be able to do during their K–12 years and write it down.
2. Take the written down expectations and throw them away.

The hardest thing to do is not expect a child or student to be able to do anything you think they should be doing or capable of doing. As long as you have an expectation, you will not be able to truly listen to the child or understand who they really are.

Creating an individual-centered environment is exactly what it sounds like. It is an environment where everything is shaped by who the individual is. If there is more than one, then it is shaped to fit all of them and created by the group.

Remember, who they are is more important than who you think they should be. By accepting the child for who they are, you will see drastic changes in how they interact with you. Inevitably, you will also find that they are much more capable than you thought they were, just in a different way.

6
Simplicity Structured

Introduction

One of the biggest changes that parents and teachers will have to make with No-Influence Mentoring, is moving from a complexity structured model to a simplicity structured model.

The best way to explain this is with the water bottle example. Imagine me holding up a water bottle. When I release it, everyone knows which direction it will head. Down! Simplicity structured means when we teach, we try to ensure what we teach is something that everyone can see and understand.

Knowing which way the water bottle will go when released is not only something everyone can see, but it is so obvious that no one has to think about it (unless you are a smart-aleck kid in the back of the room). The goal of No-Influence Mentoring is to minimize the amount of thinking the students must do.

The idea with the water bottle is that no decision needs to be made; the bottle will only fall in one direction. The goal of the teacher in a simplicity structured environment is to try to ensure that whenever they talk with students, the students do not have to think about what they were told or make a decision on what to do after (see chapter 8 for more information on learning without thinking).

You will also notice that when something is simple, very few words need to be said to help someone understand. In the example of the water bottle, usually no one needs to be trained or prepped to answer which way the bottle will go when released. This means in a simplicity structured environment, everything has to be clear, concise, and simple. In this way, the leadership model can also minimize issues and risks that people will face in learning. When things are simple, the chances that they will not understand goes down.

The complexity structured environment is the opposite. The complexity structure requires more explanation, thinking, decision making, and fewer people understand it. The biggest issue with the complexity structure is that it increases the issues that children have with understanding.

In other words, simplicity minimizes a child's risk, issues, worry, and stress. Simplicity minimizes the number of decisions a child needs to make. Research has found that when people are faced with too many decisions and options in their life, it paralyzes them and causes them to do nothing[1]. Thus, simplicity enables a child to be more proactive and helps them move forward in life.

Figure 6.1 shows the movement that needs to be made from the traditional complexity structure to the simplicity structure.

The first step to moving toward the simplicity structured environment is looking over everything you want to teach or say to a child and seeing if the idea has the characteristics of simplicity.

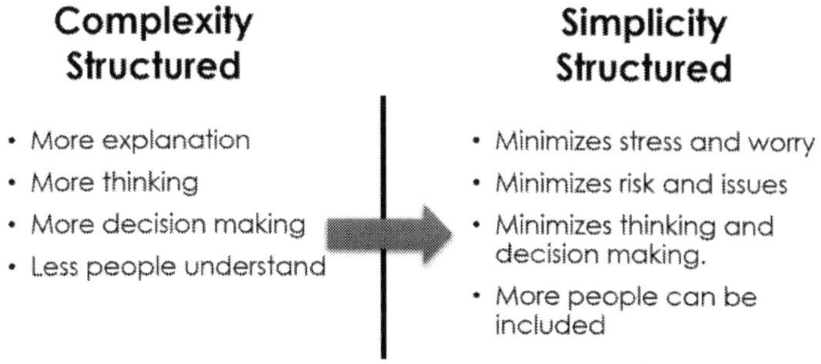

Complexity Structured	Simplicity Structured
• More explanation • More thinking • More decision making • Less people understand	• Minimizes stress and worry • Minimizes risk and issues • Minimizes thinking and decision making. • More people can be included

Figure 6.1: Moving from complexity to simplicity

Moving toward simplicity is as much for you as it is for the students/children. The simpler things are, the less you have to do to maintain the family or classroom and the more time you have to focus on the individual. Let me stress that again, simplicity means less work! I was once at a leadership conference and one of the presenters identified that as leaders "We must simplify and serve instead of multiply and manage." This should be the mantra of every leader. Too many times we get caught up in trying to become more advanced and do more things and be over more programs. In reality, we need to minimize everything that causes us to focus on something other than the individual.

We have found that whenever organizations have tried to become bigger and bring in more complex processes, they have always faced issues. Toyota is one of these companies. In the early 2000s, Toyota desired to grow their business and make more cars and capture a greater share of the market. And grow they did. They began to sell many more cars, but at the same time, their quality started to decline. For the first time, they had major recalls of some of their parts installed in their cars.

In order to avoid these pitfalls of creating a complexity structured environment in your own life, the rest of this chapter will focus on the three main principles to create a simplified structure:
1. Teach Natural Laws
2. Minimize requirements and homework
3. Organize the environment

1. Teaching Natural Laws

A natural law is a pattern in life that enables us to predict what will happen in the future with minimal information. For example, by understanding the law of gravity, a person doesn't need to know what you are holding, where you are, or really almost any of the conditions around you to know that if you release the object, it will fall.

The more natural laws a person understands, the farther they can see into the future and the less information they need to do so. In other words, natural laws simplify life. The more parents and teachers structure their teaching to explain these natural laws, the easier it will be for students and children to understand and apply the concepts in their life.

The opposite of teaching students natural laws is teaching them detailed information. Details do not help students understand how to act or what will happen in the future. Typically, students are asked to memorize details so they can repeat it on a test.

For example, when I was young and learning to multiply, I was trying to learn multiples of nine. For me, this was difficult because I didn't learn the simple law for them. When we had competitions, I would be really slow. The teacher would shout out a multiple like what is 7 times 9. I would have to go through each number, 9, 18, 27, 36, 45, 54, 63. And even then, I would have to hope I actually added 9 to each number. It would take other students less than a second and they would have the answer, 63! It wasn't until much later in looking at the multiples that I found the law. When making multiples of 9, you simply take the number you are multiplying it by, say 6, minus it by 1 to get your tens digit then whatever number you would have to add to it to get to 10 is your ones digit. Thus, it would be, 54. I couldn't believe it. All that time, I thought the other kids were geniuses because they could memorize so much, but in actuality, many of them just understood the natural law.

This is much like every subject. The more you focus on helping the students understand the principle and pattern, the more the students will understand and see the value of the information, and the more interested they will become. They will be interested because it will be easy for them to do well and figure things out. It will also decrease the amount of information they have to memorize.

I have found this to be true over and over again. There are natural laws to math, English, writing, physical objects, human interaction, etc. The more a parent or teacher can focus on the natural laws, the quicker the students and children will learn. And the better they will understand.

This really helps parents and teachers because children have a difficult time listening for long periods of time. The less a parent/teacher says, the more apt the child is to hear what they are saying.

From my own experience, I have found everything in life can be simplified to a point where *everyone* can learn it. Take the subject of physics. Most people find this a tough subject in high school, believing that it cannot be simplified. Richard Feynman was a Nobel prize winner in physics and explained his belief that if you can't explain something simply, then you don't really understand it.

Feynman was a truly great teacher. He prided himself on being able to devise ways to explain even the most profound ideas to beginning students. Once, a friend said to him, "Dick, explain to me so that I can understand it, why spin one-half particles obey Fermi-Dirac statistics." Sizing up his audience perfectly, Feynman said, "I'll prepare a freshman lecture on it." But he came back a few days later to say, "I couldn't do it. I couldn't reduce it to the freshman level. That means we don't really understand it."[2]

The most important things to teach children are the simple things. Children don't need to understand complex theories to be successful. If a parent doesn't understand something, it is likely non-essential to a child. This means we must be able to teach the simple pattern and natural laws behind it.

In chapter 8, I will review the most critical natural laws that help a child achieve success. Other than helping children learn topic-specific natural laws (like math) in everything they do, adults should be helping children learn life natural laws to help them better understand themselves and where they are going.

2. Minimizing Requirements and Homework

The idea of focusing on natural laws and simplifying the number of requirements and homework we give to our children and students means reducing the number of things we want to teach them (the curriculum).

The logic is simple: Imagine you are trying to teach a struggling student. They only get a score of 60 percent on most assignments, meaning they only understand 60 percent of the curriculum.

If you try to force this child to learn the other 40 percent of the curriculum, it will only confuse them and will waste brainpower, making it even harder to retain the 60 percent they *do* know. Thus, at the end of the year, they will learn even less than 60 percent.

By covering more, the child learns less. Since they can't understand 40 percent of the material, they could potentially lose all motivation to listen and learn. In this case, if the parent/teacher just taught the child 60 percent of the requirement, they would learn more, understand the basics better, and be better prepared for the future.

We tested this theory out in a Title I high school in Phoenix (see results in Phase 4 results in chapter 4). In the Algebra I class, 24 percent failed the first-semester final. So instead of moving on in the curriculum, we looked at the second-semester curriculum and we took out a third of it. With the extra class time, we ran a review of the previous semester's curriculum. We simplified the curriculum and taught them the basic skills. The results were amazing. Not only did the group score better on the state tests but they also got higher overall class grades. Surprisingly, even though we didn't cover the "statistics" portion of the curriculum, our students did better on that portion than other students in the school.

The only issue with this model was that it caused a lot of stress to the two teachers we worked with. In their minds, they felt because we were skipping material, the students would underperform. They couldn't grasp that less would be better.

Every child is different. This is why adults must adjust their expectations of what each child should accomplish. Many times, to a teacher/parent, it will seem like students are more advanced so they should be taught more material. Usually, 99 percent of the time this isn't an accurate idea, but you might have that class/children that are in the 1 percent, so it is critical that you understand your children well.

Homework is the same way. In fact, if you teach the subject well, then any homework should be easy for students to complete. When you limit your teaching to the essentials, the natural laws, it will minimize how much you will teach each day, and this will also minimize how much homework they need.

For teachers, minimizing the curriculum does the following:
1. Minimizes the amount of class time needed to teach.
2. Minimizes how much homework is needed for each day.
3. Provides more in-class time for students to practice what they learned.

The amount of curriculum and homework you need to minimize depends on the students. The students in my example were Title I (low income and disadvantaged) so they needed a lot of help and we had to significantly reduce the curriculum. However, I have also seen many advanced schools that should also reduce their curriculum. They just don't have to minimize as much because the students are able to do more.

For parents, curriculum and homework translates to the life skills they want the child to learn and the responsibilities they expect the child to handle. However, each child will be at a different level of what they can learn and the responsibilities they can handle. You will know your expectations are too high if:
1. The majority of your communication is in regard to trying to teach them or ensuring they are fulfilling their responsibilities.
2. The child does not listen to you or does not do what you would like them to.
3. The child is unhappy or does not like to be around you or talk with you.

If you find that your expectations are too high and it seems like all the life skills and responsibilities you expect from them are all necessary, then you have to remind yourself that, in reality, the only thing that a child really needs to be developing during their teenage years is their understanding of themselves and what they can do. And the only responsibilities they need are the ones that keep your household running. Hence, if you need to teach and make them responsible for anything, make it about them. It is always tough to minimize anything that you want your child to learn, but it's necessary. Not only for your child's sake but also for your sanity.

I know from experience that when an adult creates too many expectations or rules, it increases stress, the time required to manage the children, and the amount of resources required for them. Many times, parents and teachers tell me "That seems nice, but I can't afford to do this," and I look at them and think, You can't afford *not* to do this. It is the only way you will remain sane. For my parents, they did this out of necessity. With eight kids to two parents all under the age of fifteen, the youngest being a newborn, they couldn't afford to try to expect us to learn too much or require us to learn a lot. They just didn't have the time.

3. Organizing the Environment and Simplifying the Process

The last area of focus to create a simplicity structured environment is in the physical properties and setup of the classroom or family's home. Most of the time this is overlooked. It includes everything that is physical and anything that is a process.

Something physical could be where to find make-up work for a student or how a child can access dad's work schedule to know when he will be traveling. Anything that is information or something physical that a person would need to get to.

For a process, this could be how to turn in homework, or it could be how to perform a chore in the home like washing dishes. Anything that is a requirement or is something that happens in a home or classroom that a student or child would need to know.

For teachers, this means they have to make the following processes very clear to students:
1. How to structure assignments and notes.
2. Physically turning in and receiving back assignments.

3. Accessing and knowing where important information and tools can be found (grades, books, online resources, etc.)
4. Knowing how to ask for help from other students and you as the teacher.
5. The layout of the classroom.

Most of these things do not have a direct impact on their grades or have anything to do with the student and their mental capacity to understand the course material. However, if these things aren't organized simply, it can cause students to feel overwhelmed. This is what causes them to give up even before they understand if they are doing well or not. If you are a parent, you should know this as well. Your child might not be doing well simply because they don't understand these processes in their classes. It might not have anything to do with the material.

Take time to see how simple these five factors are in your class. The easier you can make them, the more aware students will be of their standing and the easier it will be for the students to get help, and as things become easier, it is more likely they will try to do more.

For parents, make sure the following processes are very clear in your home:
1. Instructions on how to do required actions in the family— this could be chores, mealtime, or knowing when key events happen each week (like when the garbage gets picked up each week).
2. Availability and scheduling of parents and family members—this means ensuring everyone knows what each other's' schedules are in the family and for the children to know how to contact and schedule time with parents.

3. Location of physical items— this means ensuring all family members have access to and know where tools and things the family owns are stored.
4. Organizing rooms—this is ensuring the children's rooms are organized in a manner that enables them to use the rooms well.

The simpler the physical layout of the home is and the easier it is for the children to know what to do and how to do it, the more it will empower the children so they don't have to be helped and directed by adults as much. This is something that might take a little hand-holding and parental support for the children to take full advantage of. However, the simpler it is, the easier it will be for your children to become more accountable.

Conclusion

The simpler things become for the students, the less confused they will be and the more likely they will learn and improve. There is no right way to do this. Rather, it is something that you are continually trying to improve upon each year.

To start, identify what is working and what is not. If something isn't happening, try to make it simpler, whether this is the layout of the classroom/bedroom or clarifying the process of turning in assignments or scheduling rides with parents. The simpler it is, the easier it is for students to take more accountability. Start with one thing, then move to another.

Instead of trying to measure the exact capability of each child, just assume that all the children need as much simplicity as you can manage. This way, you will always be helping students more as you get better at doing it. Some might say, We need to have more faith in the students; we can't assume they need everything so simple. However, making things simple never hurt smart children. The idea here is that when you teach new concepts, you teach them in a way that when they see it, they learn it immediately with no issues. Making things simpler can only help all students, especially those who are more apt to fall behind. For the smart kids, making the class simpler will only allow them to excel and develop themselves more. It will allow them the opportunity to learn quicker and understand more.

For more activities, visit my free course at LeadAZ.org/NIM

---

[1] Barry Schwartz, *The Paradox of Choice*, (Harper Perennial, 2004).

[2] David L. Goodstein, *Feynman Lecture Series*, (Pearson, 1989)

7
Action Focused

Introduction

I need to give you an advanced warning in this chapter. The first part of this chapter we will discuss change, an idea that is very important and when most teachers and parents hear it, they love it for their students and children. Change is the most important thing a person can do, and the first part of this chapter will explain the importance of it. However, this is not the focus of this chapter. In fact, in the no-influence teaching model, we don't even want to try to change your student or child, because it is impossible. The focus will be on helping your child be who they are and taking action to support them in fulfilling their dreams. To do this, we must understand the idea of change and how people make changes in their life.

Are you ready? Let's begin.

The Greatest Piece of Advice

Many people have given me advice in my life; however, only a couple of them have had a great impact on the way I live. One piece of wisdom that has had the greatest impact on me is: **"Things that don't change remain the same."**

At first the idea seemed too simple and obvious. However, the older I get and the more experience I gain, the more I have come to realize this is the secret of life. The goal of education, learning, or living longer **can be summed up as wanting something to change**. Wanting things to be different. Wanting more money, a better job, better relationships, to see life differently, make things easier, and to be happier.

I have not met many people who want things to remain the same. I have, however, met people who want things to change, but don't want to do things differently. Yes, sometimes I have met children that think their life is perfect and want it to remain the same. However, usually these children are ignorant of many things currently going on in their life, and when they begin to see it, they realize their life is not as perfect as they thought.

Amazingly, most people want their life to change, but they want to remain the same. People want more money, but they don't want to change their financial and work practices to make more money. They want better relationships, but they don't want to change how they interact with people. The idea that if we don't make a change, things will remain the same is profound. So many people go about doing the same things every day but are hoping that somehow life will give them more money, a better job, or more time to rest, just because time has passed.

This is the enticement of winning the lottery. Many people hope they can become very wealthy without doing anything different. Unfortunately, most of them never figure out that it is not possible. If they did their research, they would realize that most people who win the lottery lose all their money within ten years and feel they are worse off than before they won. Very few people can handle the wealth of winning the lottery, and the people who were able to handle it, made changes in their life to be able to deal with it when it happened. Because the reality is, if you don't change, then things will remain the same.

This is especially true with children. They want better grades, but they don't want to change their study practices. They want to decrease the amount of work they do, but they don't want to change the way they do their work. They want to decrease their stress but don't want to change the way they think. Many students feel that the only reason they are not earning more money is because they have to go to school or because they are young. They don't realize they are not earning money because they are not doing the right things to earn money and be successful. Many people in life started making money at a young age, and some of these people made a lot of money when they were still in high school. Today, children just aren't taught this simple idea: if you don't change, then your life will remain the same.

I always ask students to imagine themselves twenty years from now. What do you see? They usually see a car, a house, a family, having a good job, and last, but not least, having a lot of money. I then ask them, "Why will you have all of that in twenty years?" This is a tougher question, one that usually gets a facial response that says, "Good question, I never thought about that before." They say it's because they will be older, have an education, work hard, etc. All good answers, but I ask them, "Does everyone that has an education become rich and successful? Does everyone that works hard become rich and successful?" The answer is no.

Then, I show them Figure 7.1 and ask, "Do you want to be like line C or line A? Do you want to be someone that stays at the same level of happiness over their life or someone that increases their level of happiness?" Of course, everyone wants line A, but the only way they can become more happy, successful, and gain more money is if they change.

They begin to realize that even though their environment might be different, they might not be in school, they might have a job, they might be in a different location with different people. However, if they don't change, they will still be forced to do something they don't want to do, they will still feel the same way toward people, and they will still be just as happy as they were today.

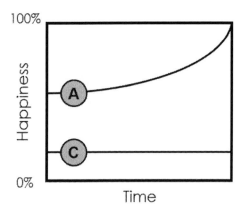

Figure 7.1: Change and Happiness[1]

I have had the chance to research and get to know many successful people. They all have found success in different ways. However, there is one similarity that seemed to be at the root of all their achievements: the ability to change, starting at a young age.

Two successful characteristics are gained with being able to change. The first is flexibility and being able to adjust quickly. The ability to change means as soon as life, work, or technology makes a change, you can make the change to move with it. Second, since understanding comes with change, the person that changes the quickest will be the person who knows the most. This makes the ability to change the most important skill to have. Now, changing is just like any other skill: the more you do it, the better you get at it. The more times someone goes through the cycle of change, the quicker the cycle will go in the future. Learning how to change is the most important skill to have. I find it amazing that we spend an incredible amount of money on teaching our children sports, chess, dance, etc. However, we do not understand and focus as much on helping children to change. A talent that will help them in anything they do, even playing sports, chess, or dance.

Success is the *Why*, Not the *What*

It is important to remember that success is not **what** people do; it is **why** they are doing it. We need to first start with the idea that certain habits and characteristics bring success. For example, it has been found that the most influential people in the world and throughout all time have all been found to utilize the expertise of others to accomplish great things[2]. This means whenever they needed to do something that they didn't know how to do, they would find someone who was an expert at it and let that person help them. This is a successful characteristic.

Traditionally, what happens is a parent/teacher knows a successful characteristic and because they want a child to be successful, they will try to force them to change and to imitate the successful characteristic, like utilizing expertise. They will require the child to have a tutor, talk with the teacher, or allow them to help find someone who is an expert at math or another subject. This will help the child, but only temporarily because even though the child is imitating the successful action, their mind is resistant to it, and when left to themselves, they will go back to their old ways of not utilizing expertise or asking for help from an expert. Actions don't make someone successful. Success comes from understanding.

There is a quote by Rudyard Kipling: "They copied all they could follow, but they couldn't copy my mind, so I left them sweating and stealing, a year and a half behind." Throughout all time people have tried to imitate actions of other more successful people to somehow copy their greatness, but what makes people great is the ability of the mind to see and understand. You don't want your child to get good grades because they were just following what you are saying. You want your child to know for themselves what they need to do to become great and successful. However, this will require the child to learn and understand. How do you know if a child understands? They will want to do and will be able to do what you ask or actions that lead to success.

It is important to realize that trying to force someone to change, or another way of saying it is focusing on changing someone, does not help them, and in many cases, we find children in this type of environment are worse off. For the child to be successful, they need to realize that utilizing expertise will help them and be self-motivated to figure out how to find and get help themselves.

Parents then ask, "So, can I help my child at all?" The answer is yes, but usually you only want to help when the child asks you for it. Sometimes, a child won't ask for help, but you might still feel the need to offer advice. If you feel you need to do this, it is okay, but if the child puts up resistance to the idea, you probably want to let it go. Remember what we have discussed in chapter 2 and 3—lower your expectations and allow the child to do what is natural for them.

Next, parent's usually think, "But I have observed that when I have pushed my child to do things in the past, my child ended up loving it." Now this very well might have happened. But we must ask some questions:
1. Would the child have eventually found it themselves? If so, wouldn't they have loved it more?
2. Would the child have found something that was better suited for them that they loved more if they weren't pushed?
3. Even if a child loves the activity, was pushing them a detriment? In the process of pushing the child, did it hurt their confidence, proactiveness, or their relationship with the parent or teacher?

In this model, the main concern above all else is to enable a child to be happy and confident with who they are. Not to change, develop, or teach them anything because someone that is happy and confident with who they are is more likely to do something. Those who do something are more likely going to improve, gain experience, and learn to change on their own. They will be self-motivated, and we have found they usually progress more rapidly than other people. They will also be more likely to find something they love to do. So, we are not concerned as much with what they are doing at any given time, but that they are doing something on their own.

Cycle of Change

This is a good time to recap what we have discussed. Change is an important part of life. If someone doesn't change, they will never improve, become more successful, be happier, become better. And, yes, the ability to change is a skill, it can be developed, and it is probably the most important skill to become successful. However, no one, yes, not even a parent or teacher, can change a child. People are who they are. The only person with any hope of being able to change is themselves. Thus, as a parent or teacher, as frustrating as it might be, we cannot focus on trying to change a child.

So, what do we do? Unfortunately, we can do very little to impact a child. However, research has identified that students that have someone that understands life, loves them for who they are, and supports them how they want to be supported, tend to be more successful and happier in life.

To understand the best way to support a child, we must understand the cycle of change. The cycle of change is a simple process that all people must go through to improve and understand more. It is a simple four-step process (See Figure 7.2):
1. Observe—A person perceives new information.
2. Think—A person thinks about the information.
3. Apply—Once the person thinks about the information and accepts it, they then apply it to their life.
4. Change—Application always will bring a change into a person's life. And the change enables them to observe something new.

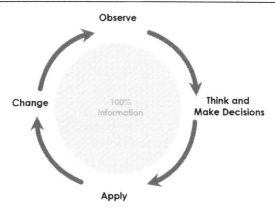

Figure 7.2: The Cycle of Learning[3]

Understanding the cycle of change helps us to understand what is wrong with focusing on trying to change a child. Even though change is important, in order to change, a child must go through three steps before that, beginning with observing or perceiving new information on their own.

For example, a parent wants their child to change by getting better grades at school. To the parent, this might seem very simple and involve doing homework, participating in class, and studying more.

However, to the child that doesn't even know why it is important to get better grades at school, they are totally confused. For them, they haven't even gone through the first step of **observing** that they are not doing well in school. To them, getting Bs and Cs is okay. However, if they do realize they are not doing well in school, then they have to go through the process of **thinking,** questioning is this a problem, should I do something about it, will this detriment my future, and even, is this something I can actually do? If they get past this step and decide they should **apply** and act and do something about their grades, then they have to determine what they can do to apply this understanding. This is a very difficult process for a child to go through on their own, especially if they don't care about their grades. Or if they don't even want to go to school.

Now when you look at the cycle of change, you also learn that the easiest step of the cycle to recognize in another person is the **Apply** step. It is difficult to identify exactly what a child is observing and what they are thinking in their mind. However, it is easy to identify if they are applying something because you can just watch them and see if they are doing it. If they are not doing it, then you know they are not applying it.

This is why the No-Influence Mentoring is action focused. Change requires application, so when a parent focuses on helping a child find actions that they can perform or do, it gives the child the best chance of learning to change and improve. Identifying what type of actions a child might be able to perform is also the easiest thing for a parent/teacher to do. And it is simple to know if they have already done the thinking and observing and are ready for that action. If they want it, they will do. If they don't, they won't.

You must remember a child cannot apply something they don't understand. Thus, you need to find the right action for the child to perform to enable them to complete the cycle of change. Many times parents or teachers will try to get a student to apply something in their life that the child is not capable of understanding. When this happens, it stops the child from learning. It is much like trying to teach calculus to a child that only knows how to add. You will not get far before the child is confused. They will never be able to learn it unless you go back to their level. This is the same way with performing different actions: to help the child change, the action needs to be at their level. Remember, you will know if it is at their level if they do it.

Action or application is an important step in the cycle of change. It is the step that allows them to move on in the cycle. If a student spends all their time on the first two steps, they will not learn. In fact, they will become really frustrated and stressed, because they will spend a lot of effort but will not see any progress in their capability. The child must go through the entire cycle of change to learn. This means they must act and change. In other words, they must do something different from what they are currently doing to learn more and to learn quicker.

For example, instead of studying for many hours, you should want your child to either, one, know how to do it and do it quickly, or two, spend very little time studying and more time going out and looking for a quicker way to get the information. This will get them to go out and do something different, and in return will help them learn quicker. In my experience I have found that students who study less are more intelligent. This is where parents and teachers can find actions that a child can do, help the children to learn quicker, and develop their ability to change.

Action is the Key

"All life is an experiment. The more experiments you make, the better."—Ralph Waldo Emerson

What enables someone to do something in life is that they actually **do** something. The only reason people are not successful is because they don't act, they don't continually *do* something. If a person does anything, they will develop in life; it is a natural law.

The quickest way to help a child learn to change and improve is focusing on actions they can perform. It is the only way to enable students/children to learn quicker, become more accountable, and improve their lives. It also is the best way to simplify life for the child. When you realize you are just helping a child move forward, you no longer have to worry about trying to educate the child in all the different things of this complicated world. You no longer have to worry that they are learning math, English, history, computers, music, socializing, etc. The child also doesn't have to worry about trying to figure all these things out. They only have to work on learning to act, to **do** something. This allows them to focus on one thing. They will still have to go to school, they will still have to learn all the subjects, they will still have to live their life. However, without the stress and worry that "If I don't do well in everything, my life will be ruined!"

This might be a confusing idea. You might be asking "How?" "What do you mean all they have to do is act?" In this section, I will try to break down the logic to help you understand what this means and how to apply it to your individual classroom or family.

To begin, we need to realize that action focused doesn't mean we want to *force* the child to do things. It means we want the *child* to act on their own accord. It means we want to help the child find actions that they are interested in. We want to enable the child to grow in their own way and in their own time. This is an important point to remember.

Action Focused Implementation

Now that we understand it is only through action that a child will learn to change and improve, let's review how this works.

This **principle** of No-Influence Mentoring is the simplest, but it's also the most difficult and it must be done after the first two principles (individual centered and simplicity structured) have been exercised. Once you know the child and understand who they are, then you simply ask the child what they want to do and give them good ideas on what they *can* do.

The following are the usual steps to helping a student act and move:
1. Education. This is the touchiest step. We want to educate the child on change and the importance of it, helping the child understand that the more they act, the quicker they will progress. Depending on the child, this step might need to be skipped or you might spend a little time on this step. You will need to be very aware of your child. If they want it, we go through this step; if they resist, then that is the sign that you skip it. Yes, that means the child will have to learn the importance of it the tougher way, through life and their actions. Some kids need to learn the tough way. Remember, attention spans are short (even for teenagers), so if they want it, you will probably want to spend no more than ten minutes at one time teaching. You also might break it up into multiple sessions.
2. Find out something the student is interested in.
3. Identify something they can do differently to help them improve in that area of interest.
4. Set a measurable goal that you will be able to follow-up with the student on.

5. Follow-up with the student and see how they are doing with their goal.
6. If they are not doing their goal, or if they have accomplished it/are doing it consistently, then help them make a new goal.
7. Continue with steps 1–6 for as long as you are mentoring the child.

Whether you are a teacher or a parent, if you want to help a child, then you need to find something the child is interested in. Find a way to relate this to the area you would like them to focus on. This might take some creativity. For example, if I was an English teacher that wanted to help a student complete homework in my class, I would first find out what the student was interested in. It could be socializing and getting to know more students. In this case, I would help the student set a goal of getting to know more students by working together on homework. Or at the end of each class, the student could ask someone else about the homework assignment to start a conversation.

The options are limitless, but as you talk with the student, learn what matters to them and how they want to improve, you can help them figure out good goals. The difficulty of this depends on the child. Some students will know already what they would like to do. Some will not. Some will not want to do anything, it seems.

At times, you might need to set a goal with the student that is not related to your class or what you feel they need. This is okay. Remember, a child becomes more intelligent no matter what they do, as long as they are doing something, anything! If a student were to do something in another class or area, you would also see the benefit in your class or the area you would like to see improvement.

Parents can do the same thing. If you want to teach your children to be more responsible or organized, first start by applying these principles to something they enjoy. It could be as casual as playing video games or making YouTube videos. Just make sure it's something that your child is already interested in. Teach them how to organize their hobby and take responsibility for it. Getting better at video games might require research, socializing, practice, scheduling, goal setting, etc.

You must remember that you are the mentor. Although you are listening to the child and talking with them like a helping friend, you must still treat them as a student and child. Most children *want* to be mentored, but they will only listen when they know the other person is listening to them. And sometimes you will need to warn the student against taking on too big of a goal or change their goal to something different. Many students will not listen to your advice, which is fine. Many people must make mistakes and go through tough things to figure out the right way. If this is the case, you must be patient and try to find ways to assist the student even if they are going down a path you might not think is the "best."

The Most Important Actions

Anything an individual can do in their life will help them to be better and improve their understanding. However, there are certain things that an individual can focus on that will have a greater impact on their life and show greater improvement in their life than other things.

The best way to understand this is to think of a house. The foundation of the house is what stabilizes the building. If the building is not stable, the house cannot be used because it is unsafe. This is much like a child; the more unstable they are, the less they can do. In Figure 7.3 it shows two main areas that a teacher or parent can help an individual improve in. One is the foundation, and the other is in specific activities in the house. Most traditional education and parenting will focus on trying to help a child make progress on specific activities in the house. This can be like learning to read or to practice doing arithmetic or practicing a specific sport. These are all things that are done in the house. However, none of these things will improve the stability of the house or the child.

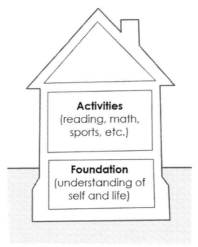

Figure 7.3: Two main areas of growth for children

Thus, to have a greater impact on the child, focus on the foundation and improving stability. This will have a greater impact on a child's capability and understanding. The question then is, What will improve their "foundation"?

Their foundation is much like a tree; roots, water, nutrients, and light keep a tree firm and strong. For a child, actions that help them understand where they came from, things that nourish their bodies and minds physically, and things that expose the child to correct ideas in the world (natural laws) provide them with a solid foundation.

Physical wellbeing
The first thing is helping the child do things that get their body in peak condition. Research has shown many correlations with a person's body and their mental state. If we are to prepare a child for living a happy and successful life, helping them to do things that cause them to take care of their body correctly and ensure they can maintain good health for a long time can affect all aspects of their life. To improve dealing with the physical body and what we usually will try to help children and students with, focus on the following:

1. Diet—what they eat. By incorporating more nutritious things and less detrimental things into their diet, you will enable them to grow and perform at the highest level.
2. Sleep—Getting enough sleep on a consistent schedule is very important. Every person needs a different amount of sleep, but usually around seven–eight hours of sleep is needed for most people (eight–nine for children). In terms of a sleeping schedule, help a child adjust their sleeping pattern to go to bed early and wake up early; research shows this is the most advantageous schedule. If they can do this every day consistently, it is even more valuable.
3. Exercise—Help a child to continue to keep their body in shape by strengthening it.

Natural laws & logic

Helping a child to understand correct concepts in the world or helping them to adhere to natural laws of success will foster change. The natural laws that I feel are most impactful are found in chapter 8. Any change in the child's life that helps them learn the impact of these natural laws will really help the child.

For example, we were coaching a student that was enrolled in one of the top high schools in the nation; the student was having issues with maintaining his high GPA due to all the advanced classes he was taking (such as calculus in ninth grade). To help him maintain his grades without having to stress and over study, we set a goal with him to talk with his teachers more and ask them for help in preparing for tests. We did this to help him see that utilizing the expertise of others will help him learn quicker (a natural law). What he found is that the teachers were more than willing to help and actually would give him a practice test to study for the real test, grade the test for him, and identify areas to study to prepare for the real test. Talking to his teachers enabled him to improve his grades and feel prepared in all his classes, which minimized his stress. This simple goal changed his whole practice of studying and allowed him to learn the value of utilizing the expertise of his teachers.

In the case of another student, we also wanted him to learn to utilize expertise, so we set a goal for him to talk with more people at his school. He ended up making friends not only with his peers but also upperclassman, who began helping him not only study for his classes but also pick his classes for the next year. They were able to identify which teachers were the best at teaching different subjects.

Personal identity

We can help a child stay connected to their roots. This is symbolic of having strong relationships with their family and friends; it also means helping them to understand where they came from and who they are. Any action an individual can do in their life that moves toward strengthening their roots will have dramatic impacts on all areas of their lives. A child can strengthen their roots through:

1. Spending more time with family and friends—many times we will start with trying to get a child to talk more and spend more time with their parents or siblings. To understand their family more, they can think of ways to serve them. Often, we will help a child make a change in their family by thinking of something they can do to help the parents or a sibling. It could be doing a chore more often so their parents don't have to do it or so their parents don't have to remind them to do it as much. It could be doing a certain activity with their sibling that they don't like. Anything that helps them to observe and learn more about their family will always help them improve quicker. This could also mean setting goals for the child to listen more to their family. All these goals can be expanded to extended family and friends.

2. Finding out where they came from—this is very similar to spending more time with family. However, the main goal of this is to help the child learn information about their family history, their grandparents, and the life of their parents. It is also trying to get the individual to learn more about their own life from when they were born, all the way till their current age. We have found anything that helps a child to gain more understanding of what they have been through and what their family has been

through helps them become more stable and enables them to make more changes in their life.

3. Following their passion—one of the ways to help children learn more about themselves is by helping them get the courage to go and do something they want to do. This could mean learning how to draw, or writing a novel, or even starting up a blog. Anything that moves a child toward doing something that they want to do in life will help them to figure out if they really want to do it or if it is not something for them. Following a passion, however small, will always lead them to being exposed to more things in life, which will only help them figure out what they want to do quicker. When a child is young, remember that what they want or what they are passionate about could change a lot. We had a student we were coaching that went from wanting to get into sports, to speech and debate, to realizing he wanted to become really strong and lift heavy weights. Another student went from wanting to be a doctor to a makeup artist.

Any actions a child can make in any of the above three categories—improving their physical body, adhering to natural laws, or strengthening their roots—will improve a child's stability and will improve their performance and capability in everything that they do in life.

Conclusion

The number one skill a child can learn to do is develop their ability to change quickly. The number one thing a parent or teacher can do to help a child learn this skill is focusing on helping the child to act and do something. Action will help the child to move around the cycle of change, decrease their stress, and increase their confidence. As Henry C. Link stated, "We generate fears while we sit. We overcome them by action."

Making this a focal point of the mentorship simplifies life for the child and enables them to realize that through one thing at a time, they will be able to continue to improve and become successful.

For more activities, visit my free course at LeadAZ.org/NIM

---

[1] Dean Kashiwagi, *2019 Best Value Approach Lessons Learned*, (KSM inc., Mesa, AZ 2019)
[2] Jacob Kashiwagi, Leadership is Alignment Not Influence, (Arizona State University, Tempe, AZ, 2007)
[3] Dean Kashiwagi, 2019

8
A Framework of Natural Laws

Introduction

No-Influence leadership helps simplify a person's life by teaching them how life works. This is the true purpose of education. The whole reason we teach the sciences, arts, languages, and math is to help students understand reality. The more a student understands reality, the more successful they will be.

The simplest way to explain reality is by helping students understand natural laws. For example, the law of gravity is a natural law. It helps us understand how things move. Natural laws enable us to predict the future without requiring us to know a lot of information, just like the water bottle example. The law of gravity helps us know which way the bottle will fall. We don't need to know where a person is, what they are even holding, or any of the surrounding details; we just know the bottle will fall if you drop it (unless you are an engineer and you believe there is a rocket engine underneath the bottle that will blow it into space). Natural laws simplify life for us so we can make sense of the millions of variables all around us.

No-Influence mentoring has a set of natural laws that simplify a student's life. Parents and teachers should try to incorporate these natural laws into any lesson, subject, activity, or discussion that they have with children/students. These natural laws are more difficult to observe than physical laws, but when a child learns them from a young age, it makes it easier for them to have a leadership mentality as they get older and it will help them to understand reality quicker.

The most important natural laws are:
1. Minimizing thinking will help you learn faster.
2. Utilizing expertise will help you change quicker.
3. Life is not random; you cannot make a mistake.
4. You are in control of everything in your life.
5. Everyone is unique.
6. The best way to know yourself is to know others.
7. Using extremes will help you simplify life.

Each law can be taught by itself, but if you can help an individual understand all of them and how they are connected, it has a greater impact on the student's life and stability.

1. Minimizing Thinking Will Help You Learn Faster

The first natural law we teach deals with helping students learn quicker. Since our focus is on helping the student develop their ability to learn, we start with the cycle of learning.

So then what enables you to go through the cycle of learning quicker? The answer to this question actually was discovered through a research effort trying to figure out what makes humans and apes different. Researchers have conducted many experiments proving that apes are very intelligent (in some cases more intelligent than human beings)[1]. They found that apes are good at problem solving, at reasoning, at emphasizing, at copying, and even at asking for help. This brought up the question: If apes are so smart, how come they haven't developed to be more like humans? After multiple tests, they finally found one very big difference between the two. Researchers found that apes do not learn from others nor do they try to teach each other[2].

Researchers presented a black box in front of the apes and taught them a series of steps that in the end would produce a piece of candy at the opening of the box. This same test was performed with children. After they were taught the steps, the apes and children were allowed to do it on their own. They were both able to replicate the process and get another piece of candy. The researchers then performed the same experiment, but this time the box was transparent. This allowed the apes and the children to see what was actually happening in the box. The apes quickly realized they didn't need to go through the process to get a piece of candy, and they stopped doing it and just went for the candy.

On the other side, the children, even though they saw what was happening in the box, still followed the directions given by the adults and went through the whole process. At first, this puzzled the researchers because it seemed that the apes were smarter than the children, but then they realized that this made sense and it explained why humans advance so quickly. When humans are young, they are willing to be taught by others; they don't try to rely on their own information; they try to learn from others. In other words, they do not **think** as much. They are not trying to use the information in their own brain (which is thinking); the children are trying to learn what the adults are telling them.

The researchers realized that apes cannot truly be taught but can only copy or memorize what they see. However, copying and memorizing only helps them if they already can understand it. As soon as someone tells them something, they can't understand themselves, they stop listening and go back to their old characteristics. The quickest way to learn and develop is by being able to follow the directions of someone who knows more. Scientists have found that only humans have this trait. It is also the trait that enables you to learn faster.

In order to learn, a person must minimize their own thinking and willingly follow the directions of someone else. You can't force someone to open their mind. The more a person "thinks" or uses their own information, the more their mind is closed and the more difficult it is for them to learn. Thus, if someone wants to learn quicker, according to the cycle of change, the best way to do that is to minimize or eliminate the "thinking" step and quickly move to the "apply" step. This means if a student can listen and then do what they hear, life will be easier for them.

Additional studies have found that people who are more successful and are leaders in companies usually "think" less or use their minds less. In one particular study with 1,500 CEOs, they found that the CEOs are most productive, innovative, and creative when their minds have low activity (shut down)[3]. This is called the "flow state." We also find this with athletes. They train before the game so they do not have to "think" when the pressure is on them in the game.

To further help reinforce the idea that "thinking" is inefficient, we compiled information from different psychologists. Their findings show that the human mind is biased, unstable, and illogical. The studies suggest that relying on the mind does not help one perform or learn very well. Psychologists have discovered the following:

1. People do not see the world as it is, but as it is useful to see (Beau Lotto, PhD)[4].
2. The brain can only focus on one thing at a time. Thus, people miss many things due to unintentional blindness (Daniel Simons, PhD)[5].
3. People do not have good memories and will believe and remember things that didn't happen (Elizabeth Loftus, PhD)[6].
4. Most decisions come due to emotions instead of using logic and information (Antonio Damasio, PhD)[7].

The psychologists have identified that people don't see well, pay attention well, remember well, make decisions well, or understand cause and effect. Basically, relying on the human mind is the worst thing that someone can do.

This is a big shock to most people. All your life you have been taught to go and "think" about it. It has been ingrained in most people that they should think more, not less. People have been taught incorrectly so their answer to simple questions is not logical. For example, if you ask people what will bring more risk when you think or when you don't think, the majority will respond that not thinking brings more risk. This is incorrect and not logical. Logic tells you when you understand something, it is simpler, and when things are simple, you have less risk.

The question is when do you have to think, when things are simple or when they are complex? Of course, you think more when things are complex. Like the water bottle example, you understand it, so you don't have to think of which way it will fall if I release it. That is what we call a no-brainer. Thus, when it is simple, you don't think, and you have less risk. This means you only have to think when it is complicated, and when it is complicated, you have more risk! Thinking brings risk!

You see this with technological advancements in society. To lower the risk to society and individuals, technology develops tools that minimize the amount that people have to think. For example, cell phones have eliminated the need to memorize phone numbers, which means people don't have to think as much due to the smartphone. It enables people to get in touch quicker and more reliably. The automated car and the sensors on cars make it so we no longer have to "think" when we drive. The car now tells you when to turn, when not to turn, and when to stop.

The natural law is that people who learn quicker, minimize any activity that causes them to think in life. Thus, they also minimize any requirement to use their mind.

When a child understands this law, they will change the following:
1. They will no longer spend a lot of time studying or doing homework. As soon as they realize they have to think, they will stop and find help or seek additional information to make it simple for them.
2. They will minimize their decision making. As soon as they realize they have to make a decision and the path they should take is not obvious, they will either go with the more conservative path, or they will go and get more information to make the choice clearer.

3. Thinking and decision making brings stress and worry, thus when they stop doing these things, they will also minimize their stress and worry and be more relaxed. They will begin to become more observant of things around them.
4. Being more observant will lead an individual to listen more to their environment and others.

2. Utilizing Expertise Will Help You Change Quicker

Now, when you tell a person not to think, this will really shake them up and the next question that they will ask is: "If we can't think, then what do we do? We sit down to do homework and we don't know how to do it; what should we do if we don't think about it?"

The answer is our next natural law. Performance, efficiency, and the ability to change increases when you utilize the expertise of others. If you sit down and don't know what to do, go and find someone who knows how to do it. It could be through the internet; it could be a next-door neighbor or another classmate. But go find someone who can make it simple for you, someone who doesn't have to think about it.

I discovered this natural law by observing older people. I was spending time with an aunt and uncle in Hawaii. They were really good people, and one day my uncle came to me and asked me to set up an email account for him, so I did. Then he started asking me about all his technology difficulties. I realized, older people are geniuses; they get someone younger with expertise, then they have them do all the work for them, and they just sit back and enjoy themselves.

Little did I know, many successful people follow this same pattern. They only know how to do one thing well, so they go and find people who are experts at things they need, and they hire them to do the work. The ability to utilize the expertise of others is a requirement to be a leader in the future. I always tell my students that thousands of people graduating college and going into the workforce are experts at engineering or some type of technical occupation. On the other hand, very few students can actually understand and utilize the technical experts around them. The person who knows how to do that will be successful wherever they go. They will do the least work but produce the most. In today's world, it is better to be able to utilize expertise than to be the expert.

Most people are not taught this growing up. In fact, many people are taught that utilizing other people is a sign of weakness. The "do-it-yourself mentality" is a very prevalent one.

However, I learned this one while I was going through college. Although I was terrible at math, I didn't know what career I wanted, so I followed in my father's footsteps and went into industrial engineering. Fortunately, my sister went into industrial engineering, and we could take the same classes together. I also found out that she had a friend who would be the top engineering student of all the engineering colleges when we graduated (so you can say she was really smart). Then my genius brother was also going through the same program. I quickly found out that by working together and allowing each person to do what they were best at; we were able to get through college doing the least amount of work. It didn't end there.

I realized the more people I knew, the more help I could get. I was friends with all the international students. I worked at an office on campus where I was friends with other student workers. I was part of many clubs that introduced me to even more students. This enabled me to get through my five-year degree program in less than three years doing around three hours of homework a week. At times I would be taking up to twenty-four credit hours a semester, and in one summer, I took twelve credit hours.

I made it out of college with a 3.4 GPA. Not many people realize that I also was providing more than twenty hours of community service, ten hours of working, learning to dance, and having a decent social life at the same time. It was an amazing time, but it taught me a person that can utilize others to work toward an objective is a person that can produce a lot with doing very little. Something that all leaders must know how to do.

3. Life Is Not Random; You Cannot Make a Mistake

Learning the first two laws in my life was very tough. They required me to make many changes to the way I lived. As a teenage Japanese boy, it was life-changing to hear that thinking and using my mind were inefficient. It made me question everything I have ever known. Second, to learn to be social and to ask for help was like asking me not to be Asian. It was tough.

To make these changes required a lot of courage, because it is difficult, and it causes a lot of fear to creep into your life. The one thing that I had going for me was the logic, which leads to the next natural law: nothing is random, so you can't make a mistake in life. To overcome the fear, I had to realize that there was nothing to fear. I had to realize no matter what I did, I couldn't make a mistake.

I learned the logic of this from my father. First, everything in life is governed by natural laws, like the law of gravity. This was an easy one. Second, as you go through life, you will encounter different types of conditions. Conditions are things around you, like people, places, and things. Conditions can also be things like time, locations, ideas, or anything that describes where you are. Conditions are always changing, but they are always related.

He explained this to me in an analogy to a seed. So, take a peach tree. In the past it was a peach seed; in the future, it will produce peaches. The past, present, and future conditions of the tree are always changing. Time passes and the world around the tree changes. However, the past, present, and future conditions will always be related. The seed determined what kind of tree would grow and the tree determined what kind of fruit would sprout.

If you knew all the natural laws and conditions of a peach tree when it was a seed, you would be able to predict what it would be in the future. The more information you have and the more laws you understand, the more you can predict what will happen.

Can a peach seed ever become a lemon tree or an apple tree? No. What if the peach seed makes a mistake and gets mixed in with lemon seeds, will it become a lemon tree? No. Natural laws ensure nothing happens by chance. You can never make a mistake that changes your identity. Everything you go through is part of who you are. Your past, present, and future are always related.

A couple of things enable us to know you can never make a mistake:
1. When you look back on an event, you can usually figure out how it happened. You can see the chain of events which link the initial conditions to the final conditions
2. Things only look like they happen by chance when you don't have a lot of information. In the instances that have happened, where you have a lot of information, you can always understand why it happened. Similarly, in any instance where you have a lot of information at the beginning, you can predict what the future will be.

If nothing happens by chance in life, then everything happens for a reason. This means that everything you do is needed and happens because of who you are—which means nothing you do can ever be a mistake!

This really can decrease stress in the life of a student or anyone as they go about life. At first, they might not buy into it, but as they observe things happening in their life and with the right mentor, it will begin to sink in and they will find that their stress and worry will go down.

Individuals learn this law as they do the following:
1. Link past events with things happening in their life (learning cause and effect).
2. Collect more information on things that seem random or by chance.
3. Talk and help others more to realize why other people are going through events in their life.

4. You Are in Control of Everything in Your Life

Once a student knows they can't make a mistake, the next worry becomes someone else coming into their life and messing it up. This brings us to our next natural law: no one can influence, impact, or control your life. Nothing can happen to you that you do not let happen. Now this is probably the most difficult natural law to realize. It makes sense especially learning that nothing happens by chance. However, with so many variables in life, it is hard to identify the cause of many things that happen to us.

To show the proof of this principle is really tough. The full explanation is found in my other book (*In Search of Truth*)[8]. For students, we usually do not try to promote this law as 100 percent true. We simply suggest that whether it is true or not, living as if it were true will help someone become more successful.

You can look at your life in two ways: one way is the "influence" way, this is the right-hand side of Figure 8.1. The influence way has the arrows pointing toward the person. This is because this person believes that everything that happens to them is caused by their environment. The other way is the no-influence way. This is on the left side, with the arrows pointing out, indicating that the person creates their environment and thus has control over everything that happens to them.

A FRAMEWORK OF NATURAL LAWS

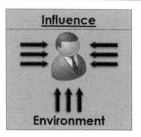

More Likely to:
1. Plan things in advance
2. Be accountable
3. Have vision
4. Listen to others
5. Think of other people
6. Be at peace

More Likely to:
1. Believe in luck and chance
2. Blame others
3. Be surprised
4. Try to control others
5. Feel controlled by others
6. Be reactive

Figure 8.1 No-Influence vs. Influence

Underneath each perspective of life, there are characteristics that go along with that way of looking at life. For example, people who feel they can be influenced are more likely to believe that things happen to them by chance; thus, they will be less accountable, more likely to blame others, and will less likely plan. They also are more likely to control or influence others, since they believe it is possible. On the other hand, the person who believes in no-influence is more likely to take accountability, believe everything happens for a reason and is related to themselves, plan, and they are less likely to try to influence others.

I like to ask the students if they owned a business, which person would they prefer to hire, the "influence" or "no-influence" person? Usually they say the "no-influence" person. Then I ask: what is more likely to be accurate, something that brings you more success or less success in life?

Of course, the answer is the one that makes you more successful or the no-influence way.

Anyone who has had to deal with children, or a spouse, will know by experience that it is a natural law that you have no influence, impact, or control over anyone. For this natural law, you might test it out to see its full effect.

Individuals who learn this natural law will make major changes in their life and how they interact with others:
1. They will begin to look for ways they can change themselves to improve their environment.
2. They will listen more and talk less.
3. They will argue and fight with other people less.

5. Everyone Is Unique

Knowing that you are in full control over your life is an empowering but overwhelming realization. To know that you and only you are responsible for everything that happens to you can bring a lot of worry and stress.

When people feel they are accountable for their life, they tend to pay more attention to how well it is going compared to others. They also pay more attention to make sure it goes according to the plan they have in their mind. And when they find that their life is not how they planned and they are going through difficulties that others are not, this is when the worry and stress comes.

This worry and stress lead to the next natural law: Everyone is unique. No two people will go through the same things in life or have the same issues. This is important to understand so students are not afraid when their path is different than what they think is "normal." You can only be you. No matter how much you study computer science, you will never be Bill Gates. No matter how dedicated you are to studying law, you will never be Ruth Bader Ginsburg (see figure 8.2).

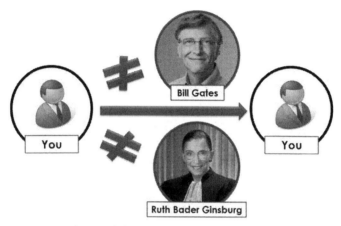

Figure 8.2 You can only be you.

Since everyone has unique conditions, everyone is different. Everyone has different strengths and weaknesses. When a person has not met many people in their life, they might not realize that people can be very different, or you might not know what other people are going through.

The more they experience and are exposed to, the more they will understand that there is no "normal," and what they are going through is fine.

6. The Only Way to Know Yourself Is to Know Others

Most people will go through a stage when they are young to figure out who they are. Some of it is brought about by realizing they are unique. It is very tough for children to figure out who they are. Many people don't even know where to start. This is where our next natural law comes in: the only way to know yourself is to know others.

Everything around you is somehow related to who you are. Meaning, since the third law states that nothing happens by chance, then everything in your environment is in it for a reason. Something that is connected with you. Thus, as you learn about people and things in your environment, you come to know more about who you are. The most effective way to learn about people around you is by helping and serving them. To serve others, you must understand what their issues are, what will help them with the issue, and what their constraints and limitations are. As you do this, you will learn why they have the issue, how they deal with it, etc. In serving others, you get to know a lot about them, and in doing so, you learn about yourself.

Many times, people think that to discover who they are, they have to sit down and think and write all the ideas in their head that tell them who they are. Telling a child to go and think about who they are has never led to anyone figuring out who they are. As you remember the first law, thinking doesn't help you understand more information and the only way to do that is to change, you will realize you have to do something. Telling a student to go think about themselves, put a list together of their likes and dislikes, etc. doesn't help them much. It only makes it more confusing and gives them more of a headache.

The student must get out and do something. It is much easier to figure out who you are by looking around you rather than trying to look at yourself. A person could also go and try different activities, go to different places, or watch different people. The easiest way is through serving others. If they just learn to help others and serve them, they will get more information about who they are faster than anything else.

7. Using Extremes Will Help You Simplify Life

As students learn that they need to understand other people, they start looking for a way to quickly help them understand. This is not easy as people are one of the most complicated things to understand in life, which is why so many people have social issues. Many psychologists and organizations have tried to find ways to identify certain types of people, yet all these methods are very expensive as it requires a lot of information from people, and even then, they are not 100 percent accurate. There are so many variables to consider for each person that it makes it very difficult for younger people to figure it out.

This brings us to our last natural law we teach. The natural law is: take the extremes. By taking the extremes, it minimizes confusion and enables your mind to focus on the right information.

The idea is simple. When two subjects are very different, you need less information to tell them apart. For example, if I were to hold up two brand new markers that were the same brand and color, it would be difficult to tell them apart if I mixed them up. You would need to study the markers and find a small scratch or imperfection to be able to differentiate the two. This would take a lot more information. However, if I were to hold up a black marker and one that was red, you could tell immediately the difference without further inspection.

Extremes simplify life because they enable you to differentiate between two things. Whether or not it is people, objects, or the outcomes of two actions, it helps you find the general rule without the need for a lot of information. For example, if you wanted to know if eating one piece of candy a day had a detrimental effect on your health, you would need to perform a lot of studies and carefully observe your body to figure out the impact of the one candy. However, if you take it to the extreme and ask if eating twenty-five pieces of candy a day for ten years would have a detrimental effect on your health, it is much easier to come to a conclusion, and in many cases, you would not even need to eat the candy to figure it out.

More Likely to be:
1. Accountable
2. Organized
3. Self-Disciplined
4. Service Oriented
5. Hardworking
6. Understanding

More Likely to be:
1. Not Accountable
2. Unorganized
3. Undisciplined
4. Selfish
5. Lazy
6. Controlling

Figure 8.3: Successful and unsuccessful traits

For people, if you take the extremes, you can minimize the need to know a lot of information in order to quickly understand who people are. For example, if you want to know what makes people successful, then you must compare common characteristics of highly successful and unsuccessful people Figure 8.3).

Take any characteristic and see what side it should go on. With some characteristics, it might not work, but for most things, it will quickly help you to understand what type of person they are likely to be.

Using the extremes can quickly help you to identify if a person is more or less likely to be successful. In many things in life when you take the extremes, it will help you to understand whatever you are trying to understand.

Conclusion

These seven natural laws help us to simplify life for students and help them to understand how to learn and change the quickest. It is never too early to start helping children observe and identify these natural laws. If they are very young, it will just help them become accustomed to the ideas so as they get older and experience more, they will be able to understand them quicker.

---

[1] John Rubin, Nova. Ape Genius, (WGBH Boston Video, Boston, MA, 2008)
[2] Ibid
[3] Steven Kotler, Flow States and Creativity, (Psychology Today, 2014)
[4] Beau Lotto, Optical illusions show how we see, (TEDGlobal, 2009).
[5] Daniel Simons, Seeing the world as it isn't, (TEDxUIUC, Champaign, IL, 2011).
[6] Elizabeth Loftus, How reliable is your memory?, (TEDGlobal, 2013).
[7] Antonio Damasio, PhD, The quest to understand consciousness, (TED2011, 2011)
[8] Jacob Kashiwagi, In Search of Truth, (KSM Inc., Mesa, 2019)

9
Conclusion

The Only Way to Change Education

Milton Friedman was one of the most prominent and influential economists to have ever lived. He was awarded the Nobel Prize for Economics in 1976. He was known for his view on stabilization policy:

> "Government can never duplicate the variety and diversity of individual action. At any moment in time, by imposing uniform standards . . . government could undoubtedly improve the level of living of many individuals . . . but in the process, government would replace progress by stagnation, it would substitute uniform mediocrity for the variety essential for that experimentation which can bring tomorrow's laggards above today's mean."[1]

Education has seen Milton Friedman's prediction come true. Both the federal and local governments have tried to make policy after policy to mandate the improvement of education, requiring schools to do better and be better. However, in the end, it has created a uniform mediocrity, stopped all progress, and created a system that no longer meets the demands of a progressing society.

The only way to change the direction of education is by individual teachers and parents taking the initiative to continually improve and change the way they educate children. The key to improving education is with every teacher and parent.

Parents have a special responsibility since they are usually the only adults that have consistent contact with a child. The education and development of a child must come from the home. It can no longer come from the school; families can no longer rely on the government to ensure a child is educated well.

The Difficult Path of Change

The path of change is never an easy one. Those who walk down it are usually alone and are usually not liked or understood. Change means no longer following the standard. This makes you different. Being different in a world of standards and uniformity is never easy.

Above that, you have to live through the change. Change means you are doing something different. Different means you are not used to it, you will make mistakes, you will have to experiment, and it will take more effort.

If you have read this far, you probably realize that even though it's tough, you do not have a decision to make: you must change. Every educator and parent owes it to their children to make the effort to improve. To provide their students and children with a chance to be more successful, more understanding of life, but more importantly to be happier.

Fortunately, you are not alone. I have presented to hundreds of schools, teachers, and parents. While I have found only a

CONCLUSION

select few that have a desire to see a change and improve themselves, they are out there. If you are one of these teachers or parents, please contact me. We can provide the needed support to help you along with whatever your goal is.

On a final note, I have found in all of my years of teaching that as I have worked and strived to change and improve my teaching to offer more value and benefits to my students, something has happened to me. I have become a better and happier person. I believe this is the reward of all people who desire to help others; they tend to always get more back in return than they give. I hope this also happens with you and every parent and teacher that begins to be more of a mentor and leader for their children and students.

---

[1] Milton Friedman, *Capitalism and Freedom*, (University of Chicago Press, Chicago, IL, 1962)

Appendix
Research History

Research History of LSA

In 2013, Leadership Society of Arizona (LSA) adapted the Best Value Approach (BVA) professional education model for teenage students. The goal of the program was to help address issues of mental instability and academic deficiencies (grades, test scores, attendance, etc.). The program was developed through four phases[li]:

Phase 1: Summer camps at Arizona State University (ASU)
Phase 2: In-school leadership programs
Phase 3: Working with diversified populations
Phase 4: Curriculum consultation

After six years of program implementation, LSA showed staggering results:
- 17 schools, 70+ programs, 2,300+ students
- 94 percent client satisfaction rating (students, parents, and administrators)
- 85 percent of parents report significant behavioral changes in their children
- 92 percent of students feel more accountable for their success
- 67 percent of students report feeling less stressed
- 55 percent feel more confident about their futures
- 30 percent increase in GPA
- 89 percent increase in standardized test passing rate

Phase 1: Summer camps at ASU

Phase 1 spanned 2013–2015. LSA developed a week-long curriculum for seventh and eighth-grade students in the Barrett Summer Scholars program hosted at ASU. The course instructors were undergraduate and graduate research assistants who previously learned the BVA at ASU.

The results of the full three-year case study are shown in Table 1. The results of the satisfaction ratings show that students preferred the BVA course and instructors over the other courses and instructors. Students were asked to evaluate their own perceived stress levels before and after the program; the results suggest that, on average, students felt less stressed.

Table 1: Performance results of the summer pilot program

Criteria	Metric
Case Study Length	3 years
Number of Students sampled	194
Change in reported stress level	-24%
Non-BVA **Course** Rating (1–10)	8.56
Non-BVA Instructor Rating (1–10)	8.78
BVA **Course** Rating (1–10)	9.06
BVA Instructor Rating (1–10)	9.60

Students were given an exam on basic BVA concepts before and after the program. Concepts included understanding leadership, alignment versus influence, accountability, etc. (for more information on these concepts, see my other book *In Search of Truth*)[liii]. Before taking the course, students had an average comprehension score of 45 percent, and after taking the class, students had an average comprehension score of over 80 percent. Upon further investigation of the survey and exam results, students provided the following comments.

"(The class) completely changed how I view and approach everyday situations. All the information that I learned through this program is completely applicable."

"I like how this class made life easier and actually happier for me, teaching me how I am in control of my life."
"I'm always trying to take challenging classes, but this is the first one that challenged me to think differently. I have learned more this week than in any other course."

The positive results of Phase 1 encouraged LSA to develop additional programs. LSA wanted to investigate how these impacts might affect performance in school settings and student behavior.

Phase 2: In-school leadership programs

In 2015, LSA researchers began developing a year-long curriculum for high school students. During the 2015–2016 school year, LSA partnered with Saint Louis School (SLS) in Hawaii to offer a leadership course. One teacher from SLS offered to learn the curriculum and teach the course. Throughout the year, LSA researchers provided material and consultation services to guarantee program success.

Researchers used the same methods from the ASU summer camps (Phase 1) to track the results at SLS (Phase 2). Students were surveyed before and after the course. The SLS instructor submitted qualitative observations as well. The program results are shown in Table 2 below. Survey results show that students enjoyed the class and it made them feel less stressed, more confident, and more prepared for the future. Student comprehension was measured by testing students on curriculum concepts. The results suggest the comprehension of students increased by 79 percent.

Table 2: Phase 2 Program Results

Criteria	Metric
Total Students	20
Class Rating	9.6 / 10
Change in Stress	-46%
Change in Confidence	+51%
Change in Career Preparedness	+44%
Change in Comprehension	+79%

In addition to these results, the SLS instructor noted a positive behavioral change in all twenty students: "The biggest take away is that students are realizing that they control their lives. It is very empowering and has given these students a self-confidence that was missing in their lives." Positive behavior is also shown through student feedback:

> "My process before taking this class was downhill, meaning I wasn't humble, I wasn't respectful to others, and it was all about me... There was a particular lesson when we were being taught to think about others before yourself. I really considered this and came out with good results. I found that when you help others you feel really good and pleased about what you did, which causes you to do more good acts."

"I've learned to utilize experts, and if you do not know something, ask. The big area this affected was my fitness. I have a good knowledge about lifting and supplementation, but I do not know everything, so I will ask experts when I am unsure about a certain lift or a certain supplement. By asking questions, it's helped me to increase my knowledge on any subject."

Phase 3: Working with diversified populations

The purpose of Phase 3 was to investigate how different populations respond to the curriculum. In Phase 1 (ASU camps), researchers taught academically successful and affluent students. In Phase 2 (Saint Louis School), researchers worked with students who showed average academic performance but attended an affluent private school. In Phase 3, researchers expanded the population groups.

Table 3: Phase 3 Program Results

Criteria	Metrics
Students	1,078
Programs	31
Student Satisfaction Rating	93%
Students who feel less stressed	67%
Students who feel happier	46%
Students who feel more confident	55%

LSA researchers offered programs to the general population and public schools for three years (2016–2018). In this timeframe, LSA worked with students from various backgrounds: affluent, lower socioeconomic backgrounds, high-performing, and at-risk students. These programs all used the same curriculum adapted to the specific needs of the school. Some programs mimicked the summer model developed in Phase 1, some mimicked the in-school model developed in Phase 2, and other programs used a hybrid approach (weekly sessions for 1–6 months durations). The results are shown in Table 3.

Phase 4: Curriculum consultation

The purpose of Phase 4 was to investigate if the No-Influence Mentoring methods could be used to improve student retention of technical skills (specifically math concepts). Researchers partnered with an Arizona high school that reported high failure rates in math classes and standardized tests. Researchers proposed that by applying no-influence concepts to a classroom, students could increase their concept retention and academic performance. The school elected to run a pilot program for Algebra I freshmen students.

For the duration of this program, LSA instructors worked with two Algebra I teachers (276 students each). Before the program, only 24 percent of students passed their first-semester exam. LSA researchers spent ten weeks (twenty-five hours) in each classroom. Researchers incorporated No-Influence Mentoring by simplifying classroom instruction and reducing control-based leadership. The following changes were made:

- Curriculum: Instructors simplified the curriculum and divided tests into individual shorter exams. Teachers

conducted a four-week review to reinforce key concepts.
- Teaching Methods: Lectures were eliminated. Each day students were given a printout with simple instructions and five-ten math problems. Teachers would walk around the classroom and provide help as needed.
- Classroom Management: students were divided into groups of 4–5 and permitted to work together and share answers freely.
- Grading Policy: all students who came to class and participated would earn enough extra credit to pass the class (D). Higher grades were given to students who performed well on exams. All students were given multiple opportunities to retake exams.
- Discipline: students who did not want to participate were given the option to sit in the back of the classroom with other non-participants. As a result, they would not earn extra credit for the day. Most non-participants became engaged toward the end of the two-month period.

Table 4 compares test performance of the focus group (no-influence class) to the control group (traditional class). The test scores range from 1–4. Both groups included similar students; all were freshmen in Algebra I who were struggling in the previous semester.

Table 4: Standardized test scores for math students.

	Total	Average Score	Passing Rate (#)
All Students	549	1.44	14% (74)
Focus Group	276	1.53	17% (47)
Control Group	273	1.34	9% (27)

While both groups of students showed poor overall performance, nearly twice as many students *passed* the test in the focus group compared to the control group. The math tests were divided into several sections. LSA students performed at least 5 percent better on all sections (including the statistics section which was not reviewed in the focus group). These numbers are very promising given that LSA only had two months to work with the students. This may suggest that when students learn in a no-influence environment, they can retain more information in a shorter period of time, thus increasing learning speeds.

In addition to their test scores, 38 percent of students improved their math grades from the previous semester and there was a 10 percent increase of students who received a B or higher. In the fall semester, only 24 percent passed their final exam. After completing the review with the LSA instructors, 77 percent of students passed a make-up exam.

[ii] Jake Gunnoe & David Krassa, *Application of Best Value Approach to Resolve Educational Non-Performance*, (Journal for the Advancement of Performance Information and Value, Vol. 11, 2019) 82-104

[iii] Jacob Kashiwagi, *In Search of Truth*, (KSM Inc., Mesa, AZ, 2019).

About the Author

Dr. Jacob Kashiwagi is a thought leader in leadership development, procurement, project management, and supply chain management. He co-developed the Best Value Approach through a 28-year global research effort. This groundbreaking model is the most licensed technology at Arizona State University in the past 20 years (62 licenses) and has been tested on over 2,000 projects valued over $2 billion, with a 98% success rating (on time, within budget, and client highly satisfied), and savings of 10-30% on all project costs.

The global success of the Best Value Approach inspired Dr. Jacob to author the No-Influence Leadership Model, a radical approach to teaching leadership skills to students and professionals. This unique methodology empathizes that effective leadership is about understanding and aligning expertise without attempting to change or influence others. Dr. Jacob has taught this approach to over 8,000 management professionals, 1,500 college students, and 2,300 high school students. He has personally mentored over 150 students helping them use the No-Influence Method to develop lucrative careers and overcome personal instability (substance abuse, family trauma, depression, severe anxiety etc.)

Today, Dr. Jacob continues to champion programs to advance the field of leadership development. He is the Managing Director at Kashiwagi Solution Model Inc., a Senior Researcher at the Performance Based Studies Research Group, and the Chairman of the Board at Leadership Society of Arizona a non-profit educational research and program development organization that specializes in leadership and social-emotional learning.

You can book Dr. Jacob or Dr. Dean for speaking and keynote events by visiting:

LeadAZ.org/speakers

Want to Learn More?

Leadership Society of Arizona (LSA) is a non-profit educational research and program development organization that specializes in leadership and social-emotional learning. LSA uses the leadership methods taught in this book to help revolutionize the education system. LSA programs teach students unique skills to help them become more rational thinkers and problem solvers. Through 70+ programs at 17 schools with over 2,300 students report that 67% of them feel less stressed and 55% feel more confident about their futures.

This book was published as a joint-effort between LSA, KSM inc., and PBSRG. Here are some of the services they offer:
- Teacher Training
- Student Coaching
- Professional Life Coaching
- Supply Chain & Procurement Services
- Education System Optimization (high schools and districts)
- Performance Analysis and Consultation

For a FREE Consultation Call:
LeadAZ.org/contact-us

Editorial Board

This book was possible because of the time and contribution of members of the Editorial Board. The purpose of the board is to review material for accuracy, relevance, and quality. The board consists of parents, teachers, and other professionals from a wide variety of industries.

Cherri Biggs	Joseph Kashiwagi
Carol Fidel	David Krassa
Julie Fishbach	Kayla Krassa
Jake Gunnoe, PhD	Jeff May
Steve Hagar	Pamela Norton
Carmen Hashimoto	April Porter
Aubrey Kashiwagi	Alfredo Rivera, PhD
Dean Kashiwagi, PhD	Ling Smith
Isaac Kashiwagi, PhD	William Wood

Made in the USA
Middletown, DE
27 May 2021